Outswim the Sharks

Outswim the Sharks

How to Quadruple Your Team's Productivity with Kindness

Reut Schwartz-Hebron

Published by Real House Press, San Diego, California.

Cover design: Tamar Nahir Yanai
Editing: Lisa Rojany Buccieri

ISBN: 978-0-9799394-0-2

Library of Congress Cataloging-in-Publication Data

Schwartz-Hebron Reut, 1973-
Outswim the sharks: how to quadruple your team's productivity with kindness/ Reut
Schwartz-Hebron

Printed in the United States of America

First edition

*This book is dedicated to my children
who came to me like the first light
of the day and the sun.*

*Thank you both for
showing me the way.*

Contents

From My Heart to Yours

Deeds of kindness are equal in weight to all the commandments.
—*Talmud*

I WAS EIGHTEEN WHEN I realized my minuscule ability to change the world. All around me, everyone was trying to get somewhere: working harder, getting degrees, using impressive words, but getting further away from being happy. Powerful people were leading nations in a direction that I doubt any mother would approve. Every aspect of my life was touched by people's feelings of emptiness. I felt the lack of love, respect, and honesty in the world.

At twenty four, I gave up a promising career as a commander and consultant for the Israeli Defense Forces in order to spend some time with my loved ones. Soon it was clear I was advancing in the very direction I was trying to avoid: waking up early in the morning to commute an hour to work, eating in the car, rushing from one meeting to the next, only to come home exhausted at the end of the day with no patience to talk to the ones I cared most about. Yet I am thankful for those experiences because they taught me what I need to avoid. I did not mind the hard work; it was the achievement mindset that was destructive. In order to get in on the race, I had to talk the talk, and walk the walk. I had very little patience. I honked at cars that were slowing me down, and was harsh to people who did not cut straight to the point.

This was my modern life.

Only a few years later, I came to the simple realization that I wanted to be happy. For me, that meant practicing kindness. Without kindness I felt disconnected, lost, and alone. I functioned very well without it, but in the process I lost myself. I decided that being kind did not mean giving up personal boundaries or forsaking a nice income; it only served as an indication of how I wanted to conduct my life.

Kindness is a choice. It is a conscious choice independent of property, time, and money.

There is an old Chinese proverb that says: "A bit of fragrance always clings to the hand that gives roses." There is something about kindness that uniquely rewards the giver.

There is more to kindness than meets the eye. By practicing kindness, people can make others want to smile, to give of themselves, and to be happy. As a Human Resources Director I found that kindness was as good for my organization's pocket as it was for my soul. I discovered that kindness builds respect and nourishes trust. And, more often than not, it makes people want to give their very best in return.

I wondered, "What if we could harness kindness to benefit organizations?"

Once I realized my simple truth, working with organizations became very challenging for me. As a competent consultant I was quite comfortable taking the lead in changing processes, but I was not happy. I had made the decision to be kind, but it seemed very few other professionals did the same. Clearly, kindness was not a popular value.

It is time for change. This change will not come about as a result of people finally realizing how much better it is to practice kindness. This change is going to be an imperative survival tactic for organizations.

Most organizations depend on their employees' intellectual and emotional assets for success. In order to stay on top of the competition, innovation, creativity, and intrinsic motivation are necessary. For innovation and creativity to flourish, employees have to feel safe. Without trust and kindness, people will not give anything of their inner selves to their jobs. It is for the sake of banking on these valuable assets that organizations will change.

The book you are holding in your hands is a guide to a unique management development plan. It focuses on the skills required by managers to train employees to excel. However, you must understand that people are very sophisticated, and none of the mechanisms in this book can be activated and beneficial without the foundation of underlying kindness. Trust me, any manipulation will be sensed and will result in some level of lost cooperation. People identify a dishonest act of kindness.

I dream of a time when kindness saturates companies and trickles down to society.

Will you join me?

—R.S.H.

Introduction

Everything should be made as simple as possible, but not simpler.
—Albert Einstein

THE DIFFERENCE BETWEEN SUCCESS and failure is rooted in people.

We live in an age of great dependency on our professional team members; products and systems are complicated, knowledge changes fast, and information flows in every direction. Managers will not win by being on top of everything all by themselves. In order for managers to analyze changes and react in a way that incorporates different aspects of reality, they need to have their team members on their side.

This dependency on people forces organizations to search for the right approaches and skills. Those approaches and skills will encourage intrinsic motivation, commitment, innovation, effective communication, sharing knowledge, and trust. These human assets are, and will always stay, the private property of employees. There is no way to force them into existence. Herein lies the challenge.

The key to unlocking these personal assets is kindness. But kindness alone is not enough. Kindness alone will not lead to excellence in a world of sharks.

And this is where *Outswim the Sharks** comes in.

---

* To find out more about the ideas behind Outswim the Sharks go to www.kindexcellence.com

When kindness is combined with the appropriate skills it has the power to harness a team's emotional and intellectual potential. At the heart of the system before you, is a unique set of human asset management techniques and tools—the basic assumptions behind most management tips and consulting advice. Managers and consultants hardly ever get trained in using these core skills because they have never been defined. Rather, these skills have been passed down intuitively from consultant to consultant, and from manager to manager in an apprentice-like system.

It takes the best organizational development consultants many years to get proficient at using their schooling and experience in order to effectively help organizations. This book is going to skip the basics and go straight to the core of management development skills. Refining knowledge that is based on years of experience into a simple set of techniques is the real engine of, what I call, "Kind Excellence." Now, the knowledge of very few can rapidly become the property of all team members, and a true revolution can begin.

In *Outswim the Sharks* you will understand how to lead people to excel with increased productivity, commitment, intrinsic motivation, effective communication, team work, and much more. This can all be gained by coupling kindness with the appropriate set of management development skills. These will lead to excellence in a kind environment with priceless results such as: employee retention, making deadlines, improved customer service, a boost in sales, and overall increase in effectiveness and efficiency. The results will come from linking the three skills of Kind Excellence, to the following two powerful goals:

- Instilling team members with a desire to maximize their potential.
- Training employees to use the skill set needed to excel as individuals and as part of a team.

These two goals can only be gained through kindness. While the core skills will serve as a compass, these two goals will be the coordinates for choosing your most effective course of action.

Most of the applications for ideas, techniques, and tools in this book are exciting in that they are different. Some are unique to the methodology in this book, while others represent an integration of well used ideas. Since it is not necessary to reinvent the wheel, I included the work of other wonderful inventors and writers wherever possible.

Some of the ideas may appear too simple. They are designed to be simple. They are powerful tools that lead to unparalleled results.

This book is written in direct and engaging conversational language. I have done my very best to avoid using complicated words and vague hip terms. I know them, I know you know them, and I find anything standing in the way of clarity a real nuisance.

The methodology behind *Outswim the Sharks* is based on a lifetime of education and experience. It is influenced by my formal education in business, psychology, and physics; by my experience as a lieutenant-ranking commander in the Israeli Defense Forces; by many years as an organizational development consultant; and by my experience as an HR director. But even more, it comes from years of traveling the globe, a fascination with different religions and world perspectives, the exposure to systemic analytical models (such as the ones used for homeopathy and graphology), and a fundamental curiosity. All this has been integrated into one comprehensive, holistic system designed to help people be the very best they can be in the workplace.

It is not scientific writing. It is, in fact, designed to make an attempt at explaining art. If you feel uncomfortable with ideas that have not been systematically proven, this is the time to say, "No thank you." The only way to read *Outswim the Sharks* is with an open mind. Decide what you want to adopt and what won't work for you.

So, if you are:

- One of the many bright managers that know where to lead employees without the "how-to" of motivating them as individuals and as a team,
- A novice or aspirant to the world of management,
- An HR director entrusted with the responsibility to train such managers, or
- An organizational development professional...

Read on!

Part I

Straight To the Point

THERE ARE PLENTY OF books out there that cover the importance of kindness in the business world. I'm going to assume that your reading this book is an indication that you know enough about the power of kindness to be interested in its power in the workplace. Here we are going to go into how to turn kindness into the most lucrative management style out there.

Problems with practicing kindness in the business world start once managers have to integrate it into the world of bottom-line results and deadlines. Managers need to do more than just "play nice" and learn how to communicate effectively; they need to lead people to results. This role forces managers to deal with a built-in power imbalance. To accomplish goals and make deadlines, managers need to have the right set of skills. Without **Kind Excellence skills**, as I call them, the first kind management attempts often fail and mislead managers to conclude that there is no place for kindness.

That conclusion is nothing more than a sad misconception. Kindness, just like any other management style, needs its own specific set of skills. Managers using kindness with effective techniques have an unparalleled advantage.

The first part of this book is a presentation of a comprehensive answer to one simple question:

What does it take to get better results than you ever dreamed possible while practicing kindness?

Part one is the only place in the book that provides you with the logic behind the three **Kind Excellence skills**. Since logic enhances internalization, it will benefit you to read it first; however, you are welcome to skip this part and go straight to the skills.

I always emphasize the importance of starting from the end, and this book is no different. By the end of Part One you should be able to know where I'm leading you, what is in it for you, and have a general idea of how I'll guide you there.

Put on your best pair of questioning glasses, and let's begin!

Chapter One

What Is the Book About?

Looking Back at This Book

Leaders have to live their lives backward.
—The Leadership Challenge

SUPPOSE YOU HAD JUST finished reading this book. What would you have gained?

This book is about producing results. The skills I teach managers in workshops do not change things. The managers do. But managers need real skills, real thinking techniques and concrete practices.

Imagine that you can clearly grasp what human asset management means. Laid before you is a complex neural network of human processes: each action leads to several responses over the network, thus making it hard to tell which response stems from which cause. It is unimaginable that you could plan an action path and know which human asset related results it will tolerate.

This dynamic picture of human asset management is full of entanglements. An entanglement can be anything ranging from an ineffective information flow to an unresolved conflict that results in a lack of cooperation—all of which lead to one clear result: the emotional and intellectual assets of individual team members being far from maximized.

Now imagine what would happen if you knew that pinning a needle into a specific spot of that neural network would release all of these entanglements and preserve the system in this "free" state. The techniques in this book will give you core skills: three such needles that, as soon as pinned into the network, will release a chain response. It works like dropping a stone into water and enjoying the ripples it produces.

As Robert Hargrove in *Masterful Coaching* wrote, "In most management books, articles, and courses, there is little or no importance placed on how you have to 'be' in order to excel at something... the typical management seminar is more likely to lead to colorful plastic binders full of information and a list of 'how-to's' than to alteration of a person's way of being."

I've seen it happen over and over again. But when managers are presented with a clear understanding of what needs to be done in order to achieve specific results, integration becomes part of their every day. Getting exposed to the practical power of the three Kind Excellence skills had quickly become the part of the everyday for Ben.

I met Ben a year after he was appointed the development director of a medium-sized Biotech company. He told me, "The last year was the most difficult year of my life." It wasn't the technical aspects of the work that made things unbearable for him. Ben was a very talented engineer, and his department was given some of the most prestigious projects.

Ben felt brought down by his own staff. "I used to love my work," Ben told me. "Now I hate waking up in the morning knowing what is waiting for me at the office. I can't stand knowing that my staff isn't going to make deadlines. I hate the excuses that we do not have enough time and that everyone else doesn't understand what development requires, especially when all I see is people running around chatting all day. At first I thought I was working with a group of professionals. I mean, all of my employees graduated with honors from excellent schools. I figured I'll let them do what they do best. But about seven months ago, when I realized we were not keeping up with our goals, I had to change my approach."

Ben didn't want to micro-manage; he didn't want to be bossy, or set himself apart from his team. He told me, "I believe it makes things worse because now my staff doesn't want to listen and share their ideas with me. I feel they do much of what they used to love to do only because they *have to* now." After going through three sessions of training to learn to use the skills you'll encounter in this book, Ben realized that it was the approach he was taking to the situation. His management skills were the leading cause for his department's results. In three months of weekly one-hour sessions, he learned how to make the changes that lead him and his team to accomplish everything he had hoped for—and more.

The feeling that there is no way to achieve success other than control and authority isn't unique to Ben. Many managers fully understand that being nice and collegial is the best way to keep people happy. But eventually they discover productivity is not picking up, nor are they meeting deadlines. Inevitably, they reconsider their leadership style—but not necessarily in the right ways.

Once you put down this book, you should know how to lead yourself and others to these unparalleled results:

- **M**anaging with time and appropriate skills for planning, strategizing, and integration. Team members are more independent as a result of their familiarity with management priorities, values, and expectations.
- **B**uilding a platform of productivity, commitment, knowledge sharing, and creativity thus enhancing intrinsic motivation, and maximizing employee potential.
- **A**chieving goals, meeting project deadlines, aligning actions across teams and departments, and leading effectively and efficiently to the organizational mission.

The techniques in this book are designed to supply managers with what their **MBAs** neglect to give them: a simple, comprehensive, practical methodology to maximize their staff's potential under kindness' rule.

Oh, and did I mention it's all very simple?

It's simple for a great reason. As I already mentioned, Kind Excellence skills draw on the power of cores, the basic principles that lead to the rest. **Core skills** are highly focused and condensed, the simplest form of "matter" that affects situations. We will go into that in great detail soon enough.

Simple, however, doesn't mean that there is no effort involved in learning how it should be practiced. Rather, cores are based on a small number of clearly defined principles. Once you comprehend them, and the relationship between them, you can stop looking at the world of human assets as endless challenges with almost nothing in common between them.

Getting training in using core skills is very different from getting skill-specific management trainings (i.e. learning techniques for

What Can Kind Excellence Skills Do For You?
A Success Story

I can't tell you how happy I was when I followed up on a workshop we held with the director of the oncology department at a children's hospital six months earlier.

We decided on holding the workshops for the entire staff because this highly acclaimed doctor felt he had to deal with a triple-bladed problem. He had to keep his interns' licensing test scores high, their motivation level high so that they would have the energy to attend to a highly demanding physical and emotional job, and still find the time to perform his own tasks well. Except for his interns obtaining very good scores, this manager was lost.

"If someone would have told me that I would be able to keep the test scores of my interns as high as they are, or even get them to do better, by devoting less time to their training I would have said that's not possible. Certainly not at this hospital with the severe cases we deal with on a daily basis.

"I must admit I was skeptical at first ... but the skills we got from the workshops have shown my staff and me that we can have it all. I'm still amazed at how quickly you came and went."

interviewing, or time management, or strategizing, etc.). The training process of core skills has its own application rules.

In order to understand how to maximize human-asset potential through core skills training, you need to let go of the assumption that certain actions directly lead to certain results. We know it works in physics and chemistry (which according to my physics professor is just another application of physics), but human beings are made of a different substance. They have will, they can use manipulation, and they hide their feelings. Stop thinking of them as we would other materials under research conditions.

Letting go of this thinking means human-asset management training can not depend on case by case answers. The likelihood of any training, or rule of thumb, covering a situation that is similar to yours is unlikely. The complexity of human asset challenges is endless. It is enough to change a single component to make any advice useless, if not even irresponsible. Breaking the cause-result chain means all we can do is create the platform in which we encourage our team members to make the choices we desire.

Guess what? That's really the most anyone can do. Believe it or not, presenting a platform instead of applying direct efforts often leads to better results. Unlike any other "material" the only way you can get human beings to cooperate in recruiting their desire and skills to excel is if they choose to share it with you.

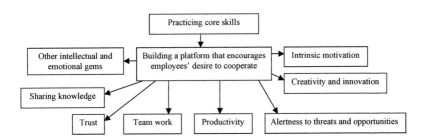

If you have been mistakenly led to think that you can force people to be creative, or that you can manipulate them into excelling in using certain skills, you are entirely incorrect.

How much of ourselves we want to share with others will always stay personal, private, and inaccessible property. All you can do is take deliberate actions to encourage team members to make the desired choices. But I can show you how to dramatically increase the chance they will make the choices you need.

In the pages to come we will explore everything it takes in order to build lasting results in your team. We'll go over a set of unparalleled skills together in order to:

- Harness team members' desire to excel.
- Instill managers with the skill set they need to maximize their potential and that of their team.

Each skill, tool, and technique we discuss in the following chapters is designed to achieve these two basic results. They are your success criteria.

Before we go any further let me tell you a story.

The Old Man At the Well (source unknown)

In a small isolated village, in a land far away where the sun shone and the birds chirped, there lived many families. The families were happy in every way except for one. Wild boars constantly attacked their homes and village in search of food. Each day the boars came and ate everything in their path.

The villagers tried different techniques to chase away the boars, but without success. One day, while the mother of one of the families worked outside, she noticed a stranger, an old man sitting at the village well. She offered him water and invited him to stay the night. During dinner that evening, the old man inquired about the chaos outside.

"Ah, years ago, when I was working on a farm six days north of here we had the same problem," the old man said. "One day a wise man came by and taught us how to regain control over our lives. But if I tell you what to do, you must promise you will follow my every instruction, even if you have doubts."

Early the next morning the villagers gathered together and, in their desperation, agreed to follow the old man's instructions to the dot.

"First," advised the old man, "every morning gather barrels of food and put it in the center of the empty field near your village." Hmm, thought the villagers, at least this way when the wild boars come, they won't get in our homes. And they did as the old man instructed.

That day, over thirty boars trampled the field. After a few days it became a routine. In no time at all, hundreds of wild boars stormed the prepared food in that field.

Once again the villagers gathered together and the old man told them to place four metal pillars at four corners of that field. The boars, ready for their daily feast, did not notice the change. They were focused on the habit they had established—coming to a field full of food and eating to their heart's content.

Over the course of a week, three fences were gradually put up around the field. The boars ignored them storming in through the only side that was left open. And suddenly, while they were busy greedily eating the villagers' food, the fourth and final fence was put in place. The field became a cage for the pigs. They were now trapped inside.

Everyone cheered. There would not be any more destruction. There would be an abundance of food.

The family came home that night and thanked the old man for all of his help. "For your kindness at the well I owe you one more thing," he said. "There is a precious lesson here. If you look at the boars you will see how easy it is to develop habits, especially the convenient kind. But breaking habits, now, that is a very difficult task. You see, the boars got used to getting easy food. It became so convenient that they ignored any alert responses to the signs of danger. We do that, too; we develop habits and feel comfortable in them. Just even the thought of change makes us uncomfortable. Only those who are willing to be aware of their habits, and change them according to need, will be able to stay away from the traps of life."

I've told you this story so that there is no mistaking in what your part is. It takes a conscious and deliberate effort to stay alert to your old habits and change when change is required. Devoid of that effort, convenience and other habitual manifestations such as resistance and fear will win. Without staying alert you can not get out of the cage you're in. You won't grow. And training... well training will remain as words on paper.

Most people do not really want to let go of old mechanisms and old habits. Not because the old habits work so well, but because they've gotten used to them. This training will only work if you are ready and willing to learn from what you see and hear, and change accordingly.

Hard work is ahead if you wish to join me on this journey of training. There is some integration, but that will seem easy in comparison to making a conscious decision to improve and train others to change.

Are you ready?

The Kind Excellence Plan

For you the essence of management is getting the ideas out of the heads of the bosses and into the hands of labor… for us the core of management is the art of mobilizing and putting together the intellectual resources of all employees in the service of the firm.
—*Konosuke Matsushita, Why the West Will Lose*

By the time we figure something out in today's ever changing world it's time to learn something new.

Providing managers with advice is no longer an effective training model. A training model needs to deliver long lasting skills that can withstand organizational changes as well as being able to apply them to various managerial challenges. In order for the training of kindness techniques to be effective it must give you real knowledge: adaptable skills and tools that teach you how to analyze, evaluate, and resolve challenges.

Along with constant changes, endless flow of information, and the complexity of managing human assets, it is imperative that a human asset management development plan epitomize three guidelines:

- **Deliver Real Knowledge**—When managers train their team and when consultants train managers, the training process should deliver real skills quickly. Human asset training can no longer be detailed analysis and recommendations, or an answer to a very specific challenge. That would be like trying to teach a child "right" from "wrong" by going over all the actions they encounter and marking each as "good" or "bad" in place of some general values and concepts.

- **Applicable to Multiple Challenges**—These are skills that can be applied with no additional support from the trainer. The trainee can now generalize them and apply them to more than one specific case.
- **Simple to Understand and Use**

The training model in this book is designed by these criteria. Take a look.

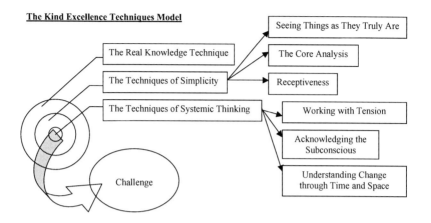

The training plan is an integration of countless organizational development principles into three easy to apply cores: Real Knowledge, Simplicity, and Systemic Thinking, each with its own set of techniques.

The training plan encompasses everything you need to know in order to train your team to excel. Real Knowledge incorporates the training principles that show you how to train others in using the first two techniques[*]. Simplicity is about analytical skills. Systemic Thinking hits on synthesis skills.

As you will soon discover, training others to use these skills requires what consultants call "Modeling." If this is to work, you will need to act and think in the same way you expect your team members to act and think. It's no different than preaching to your children to live a healthy lifestyle if you do not follow it yourself. You'll need to practice the three core skills in order to teach it to others. Therefore, I'll be referring to your own training, and that of your staff, interchangeably.

---

[*] Real Knowledge is also a core skill in its own right because it can be used to train your employees on how to train others.

What Can Kind Excellence Skills Do For You?
A Success Story

The executive director in a small size nonprofit was overwhelmed. His desk was overflowing with paperwork. "I run around all day long putting out one fire just to run to the next one," he told me. "The work is managing me."

He felt as if he had to do everything on his own. Many would feel the same way in his place. His staff of six constantly claimed the work was not done because they were understaffed and that there was just no way for them to accomplish all they were expected to accomplish. They compared themselves to other nonprofits. No one else was doing any better.

Seven months after going through two full-day workshops, the manager told me: "To put it simply we have a new slogan around here. It's 'we can do the impossible!' And we do. In the last few months we had to undertake two major fundraising events on top of everything else we normally do. Prior to the training this would have brought us down. But now, with the same number of team members, and without investing a single dime in outsourcing anything, we did it with flying colors. In the past, I had each one of my employees put 60% of themselves into their work. Plus, there were conflicts and other distractions that reduced productivity even further. Now, everyone is investing about 90% of themselves. That's like paying the same salary and having nine people work for me instead of six!"

Too Good To Be True

I can't blame you if you are skeptically reading these lines. After over 10 years of experience as a consultant, I've seen too many change processes fail. Needless to say, creating change isn't easy. Without the right set of skills and tools, not to mention a real commitment to change, it is close to impossible.

One of the most significant reasons for distrust in management development is that it is short lived. Kind Excellence techniques are different because they are designed to solve this short sighted intervention process by imparting managers with consulting skills. Instead of giving you a professional that can facilitate your change, the three skills in this book give you the freedom to do it yourself.

And here, again, doubt arises.

Can a consultant really train managers to use consulting skills? After all, it takes the organizational development professional years of studying and practicing to be an expert.

Early on, when I just began practicing Kind Excellence techniques, my clients asked: "Aren't you expecting too much from these trainings?" They tried to tell me that consulting skills cannot be taught in three to five months of weekly one-hour sessions, and that managers simply do not have the background required to analyze challenges the way consultants do[*].

My answer to this is the same today as it was then:

Imagine a world without street maps and compasses. Imagine you are driving through San Diego, California, trying to find La

---

[*] Much like the thinking skills offered in other thinking techniques such as Lateral Thinking and Creative Thinking, Kind Excellence techniques have not only proven to work, they promise deeper and faster results. For the similarities and differences between Lateral Thinking, Creative Thinking, Systemic Thinking and Kind Excellence Techniques visit www. kindexcellence.com.

Jolla Village Dr. (anyone who has ever been new to San Diego knows the torment of trying to find street X Drive when there is X road, X way, and X Boulevard all within a one-mile radius). You stop for directions and the nice people of San Diego kindly send you off with a "turn left after two more lights and then right... stay on the right lane and it's the next exit after that... " Now imagine that every day you need to find a different address. It would take time before you memorized some street names and could find your way around by yourself.

Think for a moment about the benefits of learning to read a map and to use a compass in this context. These are the benefits of Real Knowledge. You might think it is impossible for me to teach you in a short amount of time what took me years to learn. That is because you assume you will need to learn it in the same manner I did. You expect to get knowledge and information. I am about to give you Real Knowledge.

But wait, we are not done yet.

"How can you be sure I'll know what I'm doing?" managers ask me. Surely a manager needs an outside consultant to supervise the learning process, right?

Wrong.

This one is fun.

How do you think effective consultants, those who successfully use Kind Excellence techniques and other organizational and management development methodologies, know what needs to be done? They talk to you and your staff and they ask questions to find out if things are improving over time. They use their skills and human asset management principles kit to analyze knowledge in a relatively objective manner and then they get back to you. If change is required, it is you that needs to make it happen. All they can do is to facilitate the facilitator (and that's you again).

You and your staff are the key. You give consultants the information on which they base their conclusions, but you are the only ones that can make the necessary changes happen. Sure consultants use analytical skills and possess knowledge about managing people which they acquired during many years of training and through experience. But they build on the information they receive from you. Therefore, all we need to do is put the right skills in your hands so that you can begin asking those questions and analyzing.

The methodology I am offering you is unique.

Kind Excellence techniques turn the tables on traditional organizational methodologies. Instead of having the consultant learn about your organization (with all of its complexities) and make recommendations and facilitate change, you will acquire the skills to do it yourself. Managers already have all the organizational knowledge. So why not give them the consulting skills? Changing places means gaining an exceptional asset to which very few managers have access to, by achieving longer lasting success faster, and saving money in the process. And, though objectivity (if ever there was such a thing) has its virtues, a good team openly discussing each other's blind spots is an excellent replacement.

I'll admit there are cases in which consultants are necessary because some challenges do require a higher skill level. But it's much more prevalent when managers do not use Kind Excellence techniques. Using these techniques means reducing the number of incidences in which you will need outside intervention. In turn, you will increase your ability to define exactly where you need assistance and how to get it, while solving the rest yourself*.

---

* And that's how you want the training of your employees to benefit your team. You want to train them to be more independent. Just like you get the skills to break free of depending on consulting advice, our goal is to instill your staff with the skills they need to break free of their dependency on you. Naturally, it's all done with great caution because at the end of the day it's your responsibility.

What Can Kind Excellence Skills Do For You? A Success Story

When I started working as an HR director, part of my job was to supervise my staff. My foremost challenge was the high turnover of assistants. That meant lack of experience and repeated training, both of which added an ongoing load to my job. I decided to solve both problems by using my new approach to human-asset management.

I devoted time to make my assistant as skilled as if I were to perform her role.

Each one of my assistants started off with very little or no organizational background. Over time, each gained enough practical knowledge (the kind which I refer to as Real Knowledge) within five months to rise straight to a management position afterward. My first protégée became the organization's publicity and outreach director, the second was offered a position as the director of a new school, and I can go on and on. Each one learned how to manage their own time around multiple projects, strategize while taking into account the complexity of a system, encourage others while clearly stating the boundaries, and much more. All credit the training they received as the jumping board to their personal excellence.

But aside from proving that Kind Excellence skills can work at every level, what it meant to me was a reduced turnover rate, a true right-hand person that continuously became a more efficient and better employee in every aspect, and the ability to share responsibilities I never dreamed I could delegate. Each stayed a minimum of a year and a half in the secretarial position—a remarkable improvement from the average six-month tenure of his or her predecessor.

It's true that consultants, due to their outside perspective and experience, give the situation objectivity and the ability to speed up learning. But outside intervention has its downsides. It is threatening, less efficient (in time and influence), and since it does not promote independence, is often short lived. There are simply too many cases where managers should not need consulting assistance. It's all about changing the frequency and location of where you require an expert's eye and making the skills you do obtain perform at a level close to that of a consultant's advice.

In my experience, with the exception of managers whose staff is too timid to tell the truth to their face, managers can always tell how well they are using kindness. How? Simply by checking in with their staff on the two goals we set when we started off: desire to excel and skills to excel. Misusing Kind Excellence techniques is not going to lead you to improvements in these two goals. Your team members will know it and you will know it.

Kind Excellence Skills Limitations

It's important to be realistic. Understanding limitations as people, in systems, or in anything we do, is one of the most important stepping stones to success.

Kind Excellence skills are ineffective when:

- *An organization has cultural values that strongly contradict the three core skills. In this case, resistance to change will be too strong and change must start from the top.*
- *Faced with a linear challenge.*
- *Used as a replacement for firing an employee that has substantial dysfunctions and is unwilling or unable to change.*

And finally, here is the question I hear most often: "Hey, you know managers do not have free time lying around, what makes you think I'm going to find the time to practice this?"

This question will be answered soon enough. I'll show you that by investing in Kind Excellence training you will actually save time—a substantial amount of time. There are a few things I want to show you before we answer this question. I can tell you, though, that you are currently holding one of the most efficient (time and money wise) human-asset management trainings out there.

Chapter Two

Meet the Three
Kind Excellence Skills

▬▬▬▬▬▬▬▬▬▬▬▬▬▬▬▬▬▬▬▬▬▬

A MANAGER WHO HAS BEEN practicing management long enough to wonder what management is really about; a team leader who seeks consultation assistance in solving a problem but ends up feeling the process goes on forever and can't break free of the costly venue; a CEO who finds all of the advice she can muster is irrelevant to analyzing her challenge; an HR director who feels all of the solutions applied are short lived—these people, and others, find Kind Excellence principles to be the best set of techniques they ever came across.

The three skills of Kind Excellence are simple and powerful but only if they are practiced as a team. Like Alexandre Dumas's *Three Musketeers*, the three core skills of Kind Excellence are "all for one and one for all." They affect each other and are related to one another. Though each one of the techniques and principles can be practiced separately, each one enhancing productivity and human assets, it's only the combined effect that gives Kind Excellence its long lasting effects.

Why Work With Core Skills?

Let's be clear; you are in the business of facilitating change. There are the goals and results you are trying to achieve, but as a manager, one of your main responsibilities is to make people use resources and maximize their abilities to achieve optimal results.

When you are trying to lead your team, department, or organization to get a new product out you are leading a change process. Training new managers and employees is a change process. Feedback to correct a certain behavior is a technique designed to encourage change. Any time you try to create something new—a product, a service, or knowledge—you have to go through a change process whether you know it or not.

The real question is whether or not you are influencing the direction of change. In order to lead a successful change process, specific skills are required. Otherwise it is a waste of time and money. This holds true for any change process. You need the right skills in order to build a strategic plan, a marketing approach, and a budget. Each field has its own analytical toolkit. Human asset management is no different. There are management and leadership choices that will promote creativity, commitment and intrinsic motivation, in as much as actions that will result in the opposite response.

The fields of organizational development, business management, and human resources have devoted many years of research to try and identify what works in which situations. As a result, you can find thousands of models, tools, and techniques that can improve the way managers deal with challenges. Most of the time these tools are effective, but they are very specific and often require a highly experienced change facilitating professional. The world of business and human assets is very complex and, with so many details to incorporate, it is very difficult to apply the same solution twice.

People are very complex and, unlike a budget, they react. They have their own opinions and agendas. You cannot control them. Nevertheless, just like there are models that can help predict the effects of a market change (a very complex problem in and of itself), you should have access to models that can direct people to desired results.

What if we could locate the core principles of the tools, the guiding models that lead to all of the effective techniques that consultants, HR professionals, and managers use? So, that instead of trying to address commitment, innovation, and intrinsic motivation separately, we would focus on the applications that achieve all of them simultaneously?

What if there is a heart, a core so to speak, which through practice can clearly achieve all other human asset gems?

Kind Excellence Tip # 1
Focus on the Stone in the Water,
Not on the Ripples

Let's think about a stone for a moment. A stone thrown into water creates ripples, right? It is the stone, the core, the center of the circles that propels the movement in the water. It's the stone that leads to change.

We are after some stones. If we find the core actions that build enough movement for creativity, intrinsic motivation, commitment, and other such human asset gems to occur as a by-product, we're on our way to something. We'll invest energy in the stone and get the ripples as a by product.

As you will see further on, this means we have to put in much less energy. It also means we would have to isolate the core cause of change, and that the core becomes easier to teach, and duplicate.

Cores Lead to a Chain Reaction

What if you knew that by applying certain actions you would get a chain reaction, which would result in saving time and money, and being more effective at managing human assets? What would you do if you knew that by devoting about 36 hours to training your team members to use three simple skills you could immensely increase your overall productivity and effectiveness?

An effective core, an action designed to direct a desirable change, has the ability to build strengthening responses. It is by practicing three core principles, which at first might seem to have little to do with desired results, that you can create ripples such as innovation and a knowledge-sharing culture. The right cores set a platform for growth. With the right core principles creativity, intrinsic motivation, commitment, and many other intellectual and emotional assets will become a by-product. If you spend time practicing *just* the core skills *and nothing more*, the rest simply follows. By throwing in the right cores you will support a real change; it's that simple.

Keep in mind, though, that throwing in the right stones (aka cores) is not enough. Time is too valuable an asset in the world of intense competition to manage with only positive cores. Saving time and being efficient are vital. Investing in kindness requires saving time in another arena and resolving challenges at that core.

As you will see in the following chapters, the benefit of throwing in the right cores is monumental. Without the right cores, trying to establish creativity by doing workshops or building trust through an initiated intervention can, at best, be successful in the short run. Without addressing the real issues, the real cause for the lack of creativity or trust will resurface.

Most changes in organizations waste too much energy on symptoms that are the result of a core problem. You may find yourself investing a great deal of time coping, and even successfully resolving a symptom, only to find that the core problem has manifested itself in a new and more sophisticated way. Symptoms are an evasive factor. If not managed well, they will lead you instead of you leading them. Managers trying to lead changes spend too much time dealing with unresolved conflicts and other sorts of problems that could have been prevented.

For many managers, trying to resolve symptoms instead of cores, feels like standing in quicksand. The harder you try to get out of a difficult situation, the deeper you sink. Most often, the reason is simply missing the real issue. Managers and organizational development consultants alike fall into the ruthless trap of missing the core. If you do not use the right engines to promote change, or if you are targeting the wrong source of a problem, you will not get very far and the change will not last.

Applying changes at the core also saves you a great deal of time and money. The closer you are to the core of a challenge, the less energy you will need to invest in resolving it.

Let's look at a gardening example to get a sense of this principle. Assume I have a tree in my backyard. One spring morning I notice the tree's leaves are falling off (that's really out of character for trees in spring, you know). I tell myself to look into it, but I put it off. Had I dealt with it then, I would have discovered that the tree needed some fertilizer. Without the fertilizer the tree is too weak to support its leaves and drops them to preserve energy. Figuring it out and attending to the problem at that stage would have taken me ten minutes; however, since I neglected to attend to the problem, falling leaves now need to be collected continuously, which requires a weekly hour of work. Then suppose I am too overwhelmed with other duties to spend that hour collecting leaves. So, I put off that task as well. Now the grass under the tree is starting to die because it is covered with leaves and cannot get sufficient light. Do you see what I mean?

Let's look at the same principle from another angle. Imagine two of your team leaders are having a communication breakdown. They are both working on two different development stages of the same product. It is far less time consuming to work with them on their communication skills when the first signs of tension appear. It will take more time and get more expensive if they get into a more obvious, direct conflict (now you have the outcomes of misunderstandings on your hands). Additionally, it will be extremely pricey and time consuming to resolve once those conflicts turn into a deep dislike. At its extreme, you might even have to deal with losing one of them. The further you are from the core, the greater the dysfunction grows.

Kind Excellence Tip #2
The Pareto Rule

The Pareto Rule is based on the work of Italian economist Vilfredo Pareto, and adopted into the business world by Joseph M. Juran.

This principle or rule, also known as the 80-20 rule, states that for many occurrences, 80% of the consequences stem from 20% of the causes (this is typically associated with marketing and sales where 20% of clients are thought to be responsible for 80% of sales volume).

This rule is one of the principles that led to the core analysis technique we'll discuss in Part III. It is also the leading principle in working to eliminate dysfunctional mechanisms illustrating that by locating the most influential segment, you can affect results dramatically and reduce effort to minimum.

Allow me to highlight the conclusions we can draw from our discussion thus far:

1. If you identify a core action, a chain of response actions will propel the success in which you want to invest time. The appropriate response actions will occur as a by-product.
2. It is vital to resolve dysfunction at its core and as close to its onset as possible. Investing time in resolving the chain of responses to that core is a waste of time.

Each one of the three Kind Excellence skills is a multipurpose, powerful set of techniques that directly affect maximizing human assets in organizations. Remember, you are in the business of facilitating change; let us be very clear about that. As a facilitator there are two keys for your ability to direct others toward results: DESIRE and SKILLS.

A Quick Overview

Real Knowledge—The First Skill of Kind Excellence

A mind that is stretched to a new idea never returns to its original dimension.

—Oliver Wendell Holmes

Real Knowledge is not just knowledge; it is an integration of knowledge into thinking techniques. While knowledge is the processing of information (facts and opinions), Real Knowledge is the principles that teach how to use knowledge. Real Knowledge is the expert's thinking tools that can be taught to a novice.

Real Knowledge is going to serve us as an implementation methodology: a skill in its own right and in respect to other Kind

Excellence techniques. It is associated with the highest level of training available. As such, it is responsible for maintaining and developing your best employees and recognizing when something is not going to work. It is Real Knowledge that makes it possible to create managerial potential, free management time, build a culture of "knowledge sharing" in your team, align expectations, and much more.

Simplicity—The Second Skill of Kind Excellence

"What makes the desert beautiful," says the little prince, "is that somewhere it hides a well."

—Antoine de Saint-Exupéry

Simplicity is the ability to see real reasons behind systems and behavior. It is our ability to get as close to seeing the world as it really is and focus on the core. By activating Simplicity, a manager is much more likely to hit the bullseye every time he needs to make a decision. Simplicity means being closer to what is actually out there.

Simplicity is the deep principle behind the stone and ripples analogy, and it can be applied to much more than locating core actions. It is the gauge for where you are and what you need to do on your way to your goal. Simplicity is the catalyst for a well-based reaction, an ability to see opportunities and to resolve potential threats. It is the key for clarity, innovation, and creativity, and for effective energy saving efforts.

Systemic Thinking—The Third Skill of Kind Excellence

It is one thing to see reality with all the details and interactions. But creating a connection to what you see into a coherent system is entirely different. Understanding systems requires skill. It's the ability to understand how contradicting parts and other system elements fit together. Systemic Thinking is integrating numerous details. It is thinking about wholeness and being able to condense into a single thought and point.

Systemic Thinking is vital in decision making, setting direction, and saving organizational energy. It is a powerful problem solving skill which will help with effective conflict resolution and team work.

Systemic thinking is the substance of synergy; it is what makes departments and teams work together instead of against each other. By training employees to use systemic thinking tools, managers can prevent problems from occurring, reduce costs due to an understanding of the consequences of actions, and eliminate redundancy.

Okay. Now I'd like to welcome you to the part where theory ends and hard work begins. In the words of James M. Kouzes and Barry Z. Posner:

To model effectively, leaders must first be clear about their guiding principles. Leaders are supposed to stand up for their beliefs, so they better have some beliefs to stand up for.
—*The Leadership Challenge*

The three **Kind Excellence Skills** will equip you with the material needed to establish your own individual set of effective beliefs.

Part II

Chapter Three

The Real Knowledge Technique

A little knowledge that acts is worth infinitely more than much knowledge that is idle.

—Kahlil Gibran

WHAT? KNOWLEDGE THAT ACTS? Yes, that's right.

As a manager it is your role to train your team to use knowledge. This chapter is going to equip you with a new skill— an application methodology that inserts new thinking techniques to action patterns. This is Real Knowledge.

By giving someone Real Knowledge you will be handing them conceptual working tools—not digested information.

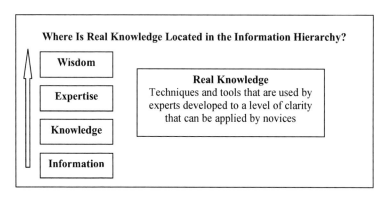

This chapter will teach you the fine points of using Real Knowledge so that you can train your team to achieve powerful results.

The Power of Real Knowledge

Science is organized knowledge. Wisdom is organized life.

—*Immanuel Kant*

Real Knowledge is organized thinking models and techniques. Real Knowledge, just like Knowledge, is based on the results of experience. Just like Knowledge, it processes facts and interactions between facts, which inexorably results in principles.

But here is where Real Knowledge parts from Knowledge and takes another step.

Knowledge is often the result of "thinking manipulations;" Real Knowledge is the surfacing of those thinking manipulations.

Do you remember how you got ready for a math exam as a young child? Were you taught to memorize that 4 x 9 = 36, 7 x 9 = 63, and 15 x 23 = 345? If so, you were given information. But perhaps you were lucky enough to have a teacher that pointed out how you could make math really simple. She explained that if you always broke it down to things you are familiar with—in this case anything multiplied by 9 is that number times 10 minus the number itself. Or, she pointed out that 15 x 23 = 15 x 2 x 10 + 15 x 3. If so, you were given a very basic form of Real Knowledge.

I view Real Knowledge as the understandings that, once acquired, make life easier. In its simplest form Real Knowledge is those tricks, the things that make our thoughts go faster on the way to reaching conclusions. In more complex cases, Real Knowledge equals life tools.

Real Knowledge	Knowledge
A single manipulation, process, or principle that applies to different situations—a mental thinking tool.	The result of complex cognitive processes: perception, learning, communication, association, and reasoning.
Thinking principles.	The results of thinking principles after they have been digested by someone else's mind.
Is always directed toward action.	May be directed toward action.
Is always complete in the understanding it conveys.	Can be any fraction of the understanding in a certain issue.
Can be learned from one case and then applied to many cases.	Has to be learned from many cases, thus being exposed to numerous incidents in order to generalize and use independently in a single case.
Guided training just at the beginning of the learning process.	Learning accumulates over time to "spontaneously" reach a level of Real Knowledge (if the student is capable of creating Real Knowledge himself) after being exposed to many cases.
Requires high degrees of time and effort from the trainer, but only in the beginning of the process.	Requires relatively low degrees of time and effort from the trainer per each interaction, but is continuous until the learner has completed learning themselves.
Deliberately decreases dependency on the trainer.	Does not deliberately decrease dependency on the trainer.
Is measured by how applicable and effective it is.	Is measured by how accurate it is.

What Does it Take to Deliver Real Knowledge?

It's not what is poured into a student that counts, but what is planted.
—Linda Conway

For kindness to lead to excellence and to maximizing human asset potential, managers have to redefine their role. In order to harness employees' desire to excel and give team members the individual skills they need in order to maximize their potential, first and foremost managers should be trainers.

Consider the difference between giving a child Real Knowledge instead of regular old knowledge when they first learn to play chess. If they learn with a pro, they are likely to be asked to plan their way to the king with each step, anticipating the chain of reactions for each step they make. These thinking techniques lead to acquiring skills like planning, weighing different options, and analyzing a considerable amount of information. It goes slowly at first, because the focus is not on the right moves, but on practicing the thinking skills. But once it's in, it's there for life. And with practice will come speed, effectiveness (in this case seeing the king out of his court), and efficiency.

Now imagine a child who learns chess through the eyes of a case-by-case analysis (which is the case when managers focus on giving answers instead of providing training). With every step the child makes, their guide provides them with the answer of how the opponent would react. The knowledge both teachers hold may be the same, but the training is a world apart. In this case the child is encouraged to learn by being exposed to many cases. The child learns the principles by acting on them. No one is guiding the child in the thinking process; the only guidance she receives is conclusions presented by the teacher. Since the average student cannot remember all game possibilities, the student has to make up her own mental rules and train herself. The mental skills this child develops are hard to access. They may or may not be effective and efficient, and once established, will be harder to improve.

In the first case, the trainer gave the child a technique, thinking tools, and encouraged the child to use them. Meanwhile, the child is making "right" and "wrong" choices along the way; the trainer avoids commenting on them until the child masters the technique. The point becomes the process. The child is first expected to practice a new thinking model. It is only after the model has been completely absorbed that the trainer leaves the technique aside and, starts evaluating the child's decisions. The results await.

When managers take on the role of trainers they need to understand what training truly is. Real Knowledge is a new kind of training, a new kind of teaching. Here managers are taught, for the first time, what teaching that facilitates learning is truly all about.

The immense education system in this country teaches people how to do quantum physics (well, some people anyway!), speak German, analyze the syntax of a sentence, and use fancy laboratory equipment and expensive computers, but it never teaches them how to operate their own minds…We must learn to facilitate the process of learning. Rather than merely accumulating new theories and more information that will be outmoded in a few years, our focus must shift to how to learn…
—Dawna Markeova, Ph.D. The Open Mind

It's not easy. But it can and should be done!

And when you do, once you understand how to take on the role of a trainer by using cores and delivering skills, results will follow. The first result is that applied learning in one challenge translates into effective thinking skills in many other areas.

One might think chess skills are only chess related, but I could easily show you how these skills can be generalized to plan and strategize in other arenas. Similarly, mastering the three Real Knowledge skills of Kind Excellence means many by-product skills. As you focus on Real Knowledge, Simplicity, and Systemic Thinking, you gain other superb skills like an ability to plan and prioritize, enhanced communication skills, project management skills and many other capabilities. That's the power that comes from combining top training techniques with core skills.

Is this all making sense so far?

As you read through the next few pages doubts may arise. Thoughts like, "If I had time to talk and chat all day I could get twice the work done." may come up. Furthermore, it is very common that the first reaction to the idea of employee independence may raise a deep fear of becoming unneeded. Just stay with me. I promise the answers to these doubts will be crystal clear by the end of this part.

Real Knowledge is made up of three components:

- A technique
- A process
- An awareness of where the learner is in the process

If you want to enjoy the outcome of this chapter, mark your coordinates as the internalization and application of new thinking techniques. Look north to your mind as we experience the adventure of activating Real Knowledge.

Deliver Technique

Learning is partly a teacher's job.

By leaving learning up to the learner, as most training and

teaching methodologies do, we are not practicing Real Knowledge technique. As Hector Berlioz put it, "Time is a great teacher, but unfortunately it kills all its pupils." Some learn fast by themselves, which is rare, and some do not, despite your best efforts (the later are the kind that are probably better off working in a different place, I'm afraid).

Do not assume that your employees naturally own Real Knowledge. It's not in anyone's second nature to evaluate the progress of a project as an ongoing process. A beginner does not always know how to plan his time and alert you to the fact that he has too much on his plate. Neither is it obvious which questions need to be asked, where an employee needs to make his own decision, or be able to anticipate progress in respect to given deadlines. It is very rare for one to intuitively know how to share feedback. People hardly ever recognize their limitations or know when to ask for help. These are but a few missing skills that are calling out for guidance.

These are all moments in which you should turn into the mode of chess professional trainer rather than providing the answers.

How?

By delivering technique and replacing answers with training.

These are golden opportunities to teach core skills. All you have to do is pay attention to any behavior that could provide you with an opportunity to bring up one of the techniques in this book—and apply it.

Let's say your team is not making progress on a particular project according to schedule. Instead of telling them what is not working or asking them what went wrong, this time you will actually use this as an opportunity to train them to use Simplicity and give them skills.

Next time, instead of responding to a question such as, "No

matter what I try, I can't seem to increase insurance policy sales, what should I do?" with, "Let me see..." and "perhaps you should... " Stop and replace advice with techniques. Plug in Simplicity and Systemic Thinking tools.

Remember, by giving an answer to a question you are teaching your employee that you are the person to provide answers. Without the skills for thinking a challenge through, all they have gained is a specific answer to a specific challenge. By training team members to us these skills, like you would before giving them the answer, you are training them to apply principles to many different situations.

Do not give answers; give skills.

Master the Process Before Looking at Results

Internalizing new thinking skills requires more than drawing on memory. It requires practice, and practice takes time. It's one thing to understand how something is done in theory, and a whole other thing to master it. By using Real Knowledge, the goal is to bring learning about from a deep place, that of personal experience. "Implanting" new thinking processes is an extremely valuable and delicate venue. And if you are going to do it right you will need to work with the right expectations.

As you give your employees new understandings by helping them reshape their thinking processes around new skills, your goal is to engage them in this practice often and notice the progress they make in using it. They do not need to reach the same conclusions you would if you were in their place. They need to master the thinking patterns in the same order as you would. If you are approaching a challenge by weighing certain values at specific weights, and taking specific steps to work through it, then you want your staff to activate the same working steps in the learning process, thus weighing the same decision criteria. That's what it means to focus on the process, that is in other words, the technique of learning. That will hold true until your team members know your process well enough to make adjustments or help you improve it.

How can you activate the same thinking patterns you're using in a novice?

You talk about the thinking process and bring it to the surface, that's how.

Try it the next time one of your staff is working through a challenge, it might be planning an upcoming project, or looking back to learn from a task that is already complete. Begin a dialogue about how they think the issue through and how, and in which conceptual steps you approach the problem. What is guiding them? What is important to you? As we go through the other two core Kind Excellence skills you will be able to add those into this discussion, too.

Focusing on the process means helping people integrate new skills by following up on the process. Now that the techniques are presented to your team members in theory, you should remind them of the opportunities they have to incorporate the new techniques into their thinking processes.

You can create more learning opportunities by highlighting decision moments, by reminding them of their new skill in a moment of challenge. When you offer advice, solutions, and answers instead of skills, ask yourself if you could do better by offering more technique.

Kind Excellence Tip #3
Highlight Decision Making Moments

If you ask me to name the one thing that can speed up learning, my answer will unquestionably be opportunities. The more chances you get to practice something, the higher the likelihood you will acquire the skill.

It's your job to increase learning opportunities. You can do it by creating such moments — assigning your employee to resolve challenges themselves. Gradually increase the level of complexity and responsibility for enhancing skills.

You can also increase exposure to opportunities by noticing them and highlighting them for your employee. If your team leader is getting close to a deadline, but there is too much to accomplish in the time left, highlight that moment in time. Tell them they need to make a decision. Any time there is a pending decision, seize the moment and have your team member try out his decision making skills on it.

If you need to correct your employee's decision, do so. Make sure, though, you do it only for critical decisions, where failure would lead to disaster. If failure would lead to a critical teaching moment, rethink "saving" the employee. If you must "save" them, tell them it's only going to be so until they master the techniques. If you feel you regularly jump in on more than one critical decision per week, re-evaluate your balances and make sure you're not keeping too many decisions to yourself.

Why is it important to master the technique first?

Because investing more time in the short run is going to save you a lot of energy in the long run. Because developing skills in your employees increases their independence and innovative abilities.

Kind Excellence Tip # 4
Zoom In on the Process and the Results Will Follow

Techniques can be duplicated and applied to many different kinds of challenges. Advice and specific answers cannot. When you train people to think differently they start thinking differently all the time, not just per a specific case.

As people start changing the way they exercise their brain they start leading themselves to different behaviors, choices, and actions.

A manager who has practiced the technique of delivering Real Knowledge instead of giving direct answers will gradually wean off of advice when it is less effective. An employee who acquires the skill to analyze the core of problems before jumping into action will choose to do it whenever appropriate. These are process-oriented changes. Mastering a thinking technique is by far a faster and more effective way to achieve desired results than by any other form of action.

A child trained with Real Knowledge to learn chess will be able to reach a master's level at chess in a much shorter time than a child left to learn by observing cases. Furthermore, when trained to use Real Knowledge a child will quickly evolve from the master's alternatives to creatively find tactics their master never thought possible. An employee looking at reality through the lenses you provide is going to understand you and work directly toward your goals. And, when they master the technique and reach results different from the ones you might have, you are presented with a rare treat—a creative team that thinks together, enriching each and every one of its members, and reaching results better than ever before.

With the exception of flexible thinkers, changing habits takes time and practice. There are some natural ones out there. But, for the most part, flexible thinking is very much an acquired skill that practicing Real Knowledge develops well. Do not worry if you do not find yourself focused on the training process right away; start by noticing when you're not doing it and use it as an opportunity to remember it for next time. It will take you time to change. And when you begin training your staff to incorporate new thinking skills and new techniques, it will also take them some time to change.

It's really that simple.

Kind Excellence Tip #5
Repeat and Let It Ripen

People vary in how flexible and open they are to emotional and intellectual change. For some, the process of change itself triggers an emotional reaction which has very little to do with the content of the change. Resistance almost always goes along with change; you can anticipate it almost like you can expect the sun will shine tomorrow morning. The good thing, though, is that most people are very capable of overcoming resistance.

Consider the following story for example:

My husband's hearing is far superior to mine, thus he suffers from noises I don't hear. In our old apartment in Berkeley, water dripped from the shower tap for a good half an hour after showering. It was the type of shower that required you to pull a little handle to switch from shower to bath mode in order to release all the water that "got stuck" in the shower head.

I love my husband and I really did not want him to suffer; however, it took me a couple of months (and I take a shower every day) to fully integrate this new practice into my shower routine.

Changing values and thinking patterns is something that takes time. It's a process that needs to be encouraged and then left for "spontaneous" adaptation.

When presenting team members with a new idea that requires an emotional or intellectual adjustment, let the process work its way through their systems. The best way is to patiently repeat the message whenever possible (preferably in related and unrelated situations so that the repetition will be perceived as repetition rather than correction). Then wait for all the pieces to fall together.

With time and proper Real Knowledge, deliberate support, and follow-up, most people learn to recognize the feeling of a new idea ripening. It is then that their emotional and intellectual flexibility increases.

Make the Path for the Trading Places Effect

Finally, you need to take steps to make sure that Real Knowledge is leaving your capable hands and getting repositioned comfortably in your team's confident hands. Remember, you are training them to think for themselves, not just copy your reactions without understanding them. Your goal is to make yourself progressively less needed. (If you are thinking, "Yeah, right!" skip to the section about what you need to watch out for).

Your ability to move aside and see your knowledge in action requires that you give direction and *focus on the process*. And finally, you will need to recognize the stages of learning so that you can know when to let go.

Watching your trainee's steps is important because, though we all want to encourage independence, we are also often too eager to help. Often, this means we do not know when it's time to let go. By prolonging our presence we reinforce dependency. Whether it's for a need of control, a desire to feel needed, or for other reasons, many fall in this trap. Watch for the signs and, once you see the baton has been grabbed, be prepared to let go.

With time (my experience is anything between four weeks and three months of weekly one-hour training meetings per individual employee) the process of trading places comes into effect. It is a gradual process in which the employee comes to own the same work process and cores that you own. Follow the next stepping stones to identify progress:

- **The first stage—The trainee is passively taking in the technique.** This stage is characterized by the employees spending most of their time asking questions about the technique itself. Here it's your job to repeat and clarify the tools until the theoretical part is clearly understood. You want to expose your employees to one technique at a time, until you notice that they have moved to the second stage. The trainee could be asking you to clarify the technique or to repeat the order of actions you described.

- **The second stage—The trainee is questioning the technique.** This is the first change you will notice. Your employees move from the details of the technique and start asking the deep questions that reflect mastery. They can now bring up new information and present you with challenges to the way you do things. They are looking for logical reasoning for the way things are and how they could be better. It's time to start adding more techniques, and applying the same technique to more cases in order to generalize and internalize learning.

- **The final stage—Change is internalized.** The employee starts looking at the world through your eyes. They have started evaluating situations by negotiating with yours and their opinions. They already know where you will disagree and will come to discuss those sensitive issues with you. You will start hearing your employee say things like, "I thought I should answer 'X', but I realized that you would probably tell me 'Y' and I need to discuss it with you." When you reach this stage, you have reached your Real Knowledge training goals. The transfer of the baton is complete.

Remember to focus on the process. Your job is to repeat the technique whenever possible. You facilitate learning. The speed isn't determined by the teacher, it's a learners pace.

What to Watch Out For

There are two main Real Knowledge obstacles. These are thinking patterns. In other words, mechanisms which infiltrate your system in the form of basic assumptions you hold about the world of business. It has been pumped into your veins for a long time, and in order to better your chances of practicing Real Knowledge, you will need to question them.

I call them the "I'd rather do something than waste my time talking," and "What will I do then?" obstacles.

Many managers perceive the process aspects of their job to be a waste of time. When mismanaged, process aspects of team work are a waste of time. But that's only true when the team does not know how to make use of process resources. In this thinking pattern, the unfortunate conclusion managers come to is always the same: planning, meeting, talking, training, and many other such "soft" practices are a bad use of valuable time.

This phenomenon takes on many forms. Do you ever want to hear conclusions before you get a change to understand an issue? Do you ever start a project without a plan? Are you really eager for meetings to be over so you can return to work? Do you find you have very little time to plan because you're overwhelmed with things to do? All of these are a result of the different stages of wanting to be in an active mode all the time.

If any of these situations ring true, then you are suffering from "I'd rather do, than waste my time talking" symptoms. You might be a member of a large group of managers who have never been given the skills to manipulate process in their own favor. This is a result of one of the leading messages the 21st century offers the industry: work as fast as you can deliver. Consequently, people start focusing on results, thinking that since results matter, moving everything else out of the way will be the best, shortest, and fastest way to achieve them.

Kind Excellence Tip # 6
Make Time to Save Time

The sooner you resolve a potential problem, the less energy you will have to devote to resolving it. Anticipating and preventing problems before they come up is the most time and cost efficient way of handling problems. It is always more cost effective to treat a problem closer to the core; because once it starts evolving it has additional effects on other aspects.

Prevention has different forms. It can be in the shape of a proactive change in a marketing strategy or when a change in the market is anticipated, a good recruit,* or resolving a conflict at its early stages.

Many managers feel that devoting time to training or planning is time they don't have. At a given moment all they can see is the work they have to do right now, and so instead of investing in prevention they insist they do not have time. Prevention in this case, in the shape of planning or training someone else to do some of what they do, would free their time. Whereas avoiding training would result in giving the answers themselves, increasing the dependency on them even more, making more work for themselves, and making this vicious cycle more permanent. In many ways neglecting to make time to save time results in an increasingly bigger and bigger problem.

*The recruiting process is considered one of the most costly processes in organizations. Not so much because the process of interviewing is expensive, but because a poorly chosen recruit costs training, time wasted on the wrong employee, the cost of a new recruit, and much more.

In the short run, that's true. Focusing on results will lead to faster results. But if you look into the future, that is completely wrong.

Focusing on a training process instead of focusing on results will save you even more time—in the long run.

I'm serious. You did not misunderstand me. I really mean it.

This is one of the most common misconceptions about training. Managers stuck on local optimization think they save time by focusing on accomplishing the tasks at hand. But in actuality, looking only far enough to see the end of their nose is going to make them spend more time, not less.

Just like you need to overcome this misconception to practice Real Knowledge, so does your team.

Consider that if your employees worked for other companies before landing in your team, the conditioning to allocating time for learning was probably nonexistent. New employees are expected to jump right in and swim. Since everyone is stuck in the same pond, each team member busier than the next, there is no time to teach and no time to learn. Baptism by fire is a common welcome.

I've worked with brilliant team members and managers who feel paralyzed when asked to resolve something themselves, especially when their supervisor can just give them the answer. And you and I both know very few people have patience to learn anything anymore. In the age of computers, with everything speeding up, we want instant answers.

You might find your employees impatient with your Real Knowledge training. They have work to do and there is really no time. Unfortunately there is never time, except for retreats and workshops, and these are too few and often too late to be truly helpful.

Why should a staff member think about the alternative solutions if the manager knows the answer? It's just a big waste of time, right?

It's simple mathematics. If you need to devote five minutes to solving someone else's challenge every day and three hours to train them to do it themselves, then it only makes sense to choose the five-minute version if you will be working with that person no more than 36 days…

But saving time isn't the only reason you should train people to use Real Knowledge.

If you want people to think as a group, you need to teach them to use Real Knowledge. Without exposing and aligning working assumptions, you will have very little influence on how things get done beyond setting direction. Direction is important, but your job is to get people to goals, not just present them with goals and wonder why it is taking them so long to get there.

"What will I do when my team members do not need me to tell them what to do anymore?" is the second obstacle you may be facing in response to practicing Real Knowledge.

Many managers react strongly to the idea of propelling their staff toward independence. They want to see their employees prosper for all the right reasons, but suddenly a strong unexplained fear takes over.

I see it as a "void fear." Suddenly managers cannot imagine what they'll do when their role as "answer givers" or even "trainers" is over. They experience the full force of the ignorance that surrounds the word "management."

I have seen this phenomenon happen with some of the most intelligent people I know—and I hardly blame them. It's a question professionals have been working on for years (most senior executives, business school educators, and consultants still struggle with this question).

Henry Mintzberg, one of the world's leading management educators, writes in his book *Managers Not MBAs*:

"Management is not marketing plus finance plus accounting and so forth. It is *about* these things, but it is not these things. Pour each of these functions, of a different color, into that empty vessel called an MBA student, stir lightly, and you end up with a set of specialized stripes, not a blended manager."

With the understanding that management is not taught in business schools, he goes on to ask: "The question remains of where the synthesis comes from. The usual dismissive answer is the students: They will put it together." Mintzberg suggests you think of this as the IKEA model of management education; the schools supply the pieces, neatly cut to size. The students do the assembly. But unfortunately, he says, the schools do not provide instructions.

This is understandable. Most business schools are all about knowledge; however, management is a profession that requires Real Knowledge.

Remember what I said about Real Knowledge? A child that masters chess thinking skills can easily apply the same skills to marketing and so on. Guess what? By applying the three Kind Excellence skills in this book, you will have the building blocks for understanding management. And though that would be taking a bigger step than this book can accommodate, working with these three core skills builds an excellent platform to figuring out the enigma of management.

Chapter Four

Practice Real Knowledge

Real Knowledge—Try It Out

BEFORE YOU IS A complex, real life human asset management challenge. At first glance you might feel a little puzzled by it, due to the apparent leap you need to make in order to resolve the difference between theory and practice. Real life challenges are always more complex than theories, and since we've already established that we want you to know how to use this and not just understand it, there is really no way around it.

As with any real life challenge this one has many aspects and should be approached by looking at all three Kind Excellence skills. But here we'll look at it by only applying Real Knowledge tools. If you wish, you can compare the ideas here with what you would have chosen to do before you used Kind Excellence tools. This may give you a good idea as to how much work you need to do on this particular core skill.

Once you have given it a fair shot, go back and read my take on it. There is no need to evaluate the differences between my answer and yours. First, both you and I could be right (I only know mine is right because it worked, and maybe yours would have worked too, we'll never know). But more importantly, as we saw in "Repeat and Let it Ripen," learning is meant to be a spontaneous process.

This is the first case study. First you will just feel you understand mentally, but it's just not sinking in. Maybe this time my take on things will not be clear, but read it anyway. By the end of the book you will know to anticipate my answer.

Let's see, what we have got here.*

There is Nothing like Experience.
A Case Study Report

Setting: A life insurance telemarketing department at a medium-sized insurance company.

"We're doing everything we can think of, but no matter how hard we try there is no increase in sales." This particular CEO spent an hour and a half going into great detail about what he had already tried to do for this new telemarketing department. Somehow, he felt all attempts made no difference. Seven months after this department had been formed to accommodate past increases in life insurance sales, the CEO was thinking of shutting it down. "Maybe the market has changed all of a sudden...I don't know if there is anything that can be done to increase sales again," he said.

The Facts:
- *Life insurance sales had increased to the point that it was worth opening a new department specializing in life insurance policy sales.*
- *The company had 2 other departments that dealt with other types of insurance.*
- *Only 3 out of the 45 telemarketers in the new department were from the other 2 departments and were considered good at selling life insurance policies.*

---

* Though this case study could easily be given as a basis for a Simplicity analysis, I have chosen it here for its obvious Real Knowledge characteristics (you can get an interviewing point of view of this example at www.kindexcellence.com).The difficulty in resolving the root issue really highlights the difference Real Knowledge makes.

- *Only 8 telemarketers (including the three mentioned above) had previous knowledge about life insurance.*
- *Each telemarketer had 2 weeks worth of training covering both life insurance and telemarketing, after which personal training was received that included listening in on their conversations followed by feedback.*
- *A new manager was recruited to run the new department. This young creative, vibrant, sharp, and kind manager was a whiz at selling life insurance policies, and had worked for over 5 years as a manager of a life insurance team in one of the top insurance companies.*
- *Motivational bonuses and other such incentives had been offered to increase sales.*
- *There had been a decrease in sales.*

A few things stand out right away. This department has a new manager and most of the staff is new. Training needs to take most team members from no background to being proficient in the world of life insurance and telemarketing. Both these fields of expertise require Real Knowledge skills. Without them, the chances of becoming a successful sales person are significantly decreased.

The CEO assumed that since his new manager was so good at selling life insurance over the phone, she would also be fantastic at managing others and they would duplicate her achievements. This very common mistake comes from the misconception that regular knowledge and Real Knowledge are very similar. Just because someone knows how to sell does not mean they know how to transform their expertise into something novices can use or manage those novices in the process of duplicating their efforts.

Training for this company consisted of studying and getting tested on the detailed information necessary for succeeding in life insurance, an overview of a sales model (creating closeness, identifying and elaborating needs, etc.), and many role-play sessions that included conversation scenarios and how to deal with typical resistance.

The material was actually not bad, and I could recognize some of it from similar workshops I had given in the past. Only there was one monumental difference. It was taught as case by case example training. It would take months, if not years, of experience to cover all cases and develop an "instinct" for doing it.

This wonderful new department manager was not delivering Real Knowledge, mainly because she was missing Real Knowledge on how to train others effectively. She presented the team with opportunities to learn. She provided tools and examples of how it was done and made sure her representatives were savvy in the details. She even provided individual team members with personal feedback by listening to their conversation recordings with clients. But she did nothing about learning. She left that for the team members to figure out for themselves.

Each learning opportunity that arose was eliminated instantly (at least as far as Real Knowledge was concerned) by a quick, informative knowledgeable answer.

We changed one thing and one thing only—the training technique (as we've already seen in the Pareto rule and as we'll see in the chapter about Simplicity: all good change should focus on a core problem). The manager was to address each question and each challenge her team had to deal with by guiding their thinking process on the surface, exposing their basic assumptions, and providing them with guidance of values, priorities, and connections to the process their client was going through. She made them practice thinking about sales in the same way she was thinking about it, rather than providing them with answers.

Instead of replying to a question with, "Sure just go tell him that… " She now started asking questions like, "How do *you* think you should reply to this?" Followed by, "Why?" and "We really want the client to feel close to you. How do you think you can get him to connect more?" By asking those questions, she is teaching thinking patterns.

Within a month and a half, sales were not only increased to their previous state, they were substantially higher, making the life insurance department the most profitable of the three.

Real Knowledge—Maximizing Human Assets

Real Knowledge is a skill that lives very well in the realm of kindness. In fact, it needs kindness in order to prosper. Real Knowledge re-focuses on the individual receiving instead of the transmitter. It requires the safe environment of trust and care that only kindness can deliver. And it needs kindness as the key to unlock the desire and skills that will lead to excellence.

As with all three Kind Excellence skills, the benefits of practicing Real Knowledge go far beyond the direct results of acquiring thinking skills. That is just the first ripple produced by throwing in the first stone. As you read through the outer ripples remember that, as with the analogy we made earlier, these by-product results are effortless as far as you are concerned. They are presented here so that you will know what you can expect to enjoy.

Real Knowledge and Building Up a Desire to Excel

In order to understand how Real Knowledge and other Kind Excellence skills contribute to the desire to excel, we first need to define what a desire to excel is made of.

If you put aside the emotional dysfunctions we adopt growing up, all people have a basic desire to maximize their own potential*. Most of us are too confused with contradicting values and expectations to know what our exact potential is, but we all want to be at our best. We want to know more and do better.

I like to think of your employees' desire as the source of fire, a delicate flame caged in our soul. You can make it burn stronger and you certainly do not want to lose it. Think about it this way: if you were roughing it out in the freezing arctic tundra, far away from any civilized area, the matches in your backpack would be like the desire to excel—you would make sure not to lose them under any circumstances. This is how precious and fragile your team's desire to excel is.

There is a long philosophical debate about what a desire to excel is made of. Scholars seem to think that the desire to excel is made out of a blend of healthy self esteem, independence and autonomy, perception of influence, and a sense of purpose. While I agree with these statements, I also believe that being more of who we really are and being successful at it is a motivation in and of itself.

Supporting self-esteem, independence, and a sense of purpose is great. But I'm sure you're wondering how it fits in with the real world. Unfortunately, we do not all have a good grasp on where we should improve, and sometimes when we try to highlight it

---

* Do note that by excel I mean maximizing one's potential according to one's own talents and passions. For me, excellence has very little to do with meeting social standards.

for others they can get defensive. Feedback can easily decrease or eliminate the desire to excel. That's actually one of the main reasons managers shy away from using kindness. They simply do not know how to incorporate constructive feedback and control in conjunction with kindness. Luckily, there is plenty you can do about it. Part four will go over the principles that allow for feedback to become the engine for growth, rather than an all around bad experience.

Now that we've got the concept of the desire to excel covered, let's turn back to the ways in which Real Knowledge preserves and increases the desire to excel.

The most obvious results of Real Knowledge are independence and autonomy and the perception of an influential capability. By using Real Knowledge as a training form, managers align their team members' problem solving and thinking processes with other team members, as well as with their own. By using Real Knowledge you come to trust that your team will follow your thought process, understand your priorities, and come talk to you when they disagree—because that is the way you trained them.

Herein rests the key to a remarkable combination; managerial control and employee autonomy. It's a superb combination for the age of knowledge. Real Knowledge gives employees autonomy. And with it come freedom, self expression, and growth. Employees who get used to Real Knowledge practices grow as individuals as they explore the limits of their own mind by taking on new thinking skills.

Employees who experience autonomy feel a greater ability to influence things. Though it is clearly the manager's place to make decisions if needed, Real Knowledge directs a great deal of control back into team members' hands. Employees get to make more decisions and are encouraged to voice their analysis in any situation the manager needs to call on. More control of the situation, and a sense of importance through involvement, are high up on the list of self fulfillment for anyone.

Take it from James Kouzes and Barry Posner in *The Leadership Challenge*. "When people have more discretion, more authority, and more information, they're much more likely to use their energies to produce extraordinary results."

Needless to say, using Real Knowledge means you will have more time (reducing dependency has this strange effect), your staff will anticipate you better, follow your expectations more effectively and, as a result of their independence, will be more satisfied and motivated to work for you.

Yet independence, autonomy, and a perception of influence are just the tip of the iceberg.

The second milestone Real Knowledge touches on is commitment. It is very likely that teaching Real Knowledge will make your employees perceive you as a mentor[*]. I bet you remember each and every person who ever gave you Real Knowledge. People usually do because such gifts are rare and precious. When people feel they are given the skills to perform at the top of their potential, and once those skills start leading them to better results, people often value it as a priceless gift. Teams who feel they are receiving a lot want to give a lot in return. That's the power of kindness for you.

Moving away from a result oriented mind to focusing on developing the people who act on them, offers a solution for one of this age's strongest alienating feelings; the disconnection between people and tasks. Most people go to work because they have to. They may enjoy the companionship and feeling

---

[*] This title is too often taken on by mentors, and in truth should be given by a trainee.

productive, but they are usually more concerned about how a particular project will look on their resume, than feel personally invested in achieving the specific project they're working on for the sake of excelling at it. If people can't connect to their jobs, then they can't connect to themselves while they are at work, and that hinders their desire to excel.

Consultants and managers can talk forever about intrinsic motivation, but without this fundamental link between people and tasks, intrinsic motivation is a moot point. Since Real Knowledge focuses on developing people rather than results, it creates a bridge between employees and their work. Employees are growing and improving as individuals. They are constantly learning new things about themselves, expressing who they are, and ultimately expanding their abilities around work.

It's truly great, isn't it?

Real Knowledge and the Skills to Excel

Real Knowledge is a training methodology designed to transform any set of knowledge into skills. Using Real Knowledge is going to enhance an individual's ability to maximize their potential to excel.

However, there are other wonderful side benefits to this training approach.

The first valuable set of skills Real Knowledge provides is actually for managers. By using Real Knowledge techniques managers can, in time, overcome the uncertainty that surrounds the meaning of management. This is undoubtedly true for human asset management. That's good because a manager confident in his or her role as a trainer, leader, facilitator, integrator, evaluator, and decision maker is going to develop a team free of unnecessary obstacles. Such a team will inevitably be more productive, creative, and maximize the abilities of individuals and the team as a whole.

As team members begin speaking the same language and using the same thinking models, team work skills are instantly improved. There are clear work standards. Everyone is crystal clear about goals and how to achieve them. In time, you will come to trust your team to bring up obstacles; including estimates about the speed of progress, how to improve efficiency, and anything that just doesn't make sense to them. This saves the manager from unanticipated issues and from wasting time.

Practicing Real Knowledge is a way to create self management and utilize the potential of managerial skills. Your team is going to start using the models it took others years to develop very early on in their career (some yours, some mine, some you will pick up along the way as you look for more Real Knowledge). Some employees will actually enjoy this at their first job. They will learn skills like prioritizing, planning, following up on progress, evaluating their decision making process and that of others. These skills are often intangible as far as employees are concerned, and often not practiced and taught by many managers.

I'll give you another example of an easy and dramatic improvement utilizing Real Knowledge. I want you to take a look at customer service skills. When was the last time you asked anyone for assistance, be it a service representative over the phone or someone from the HR department, and heard, "I'm sorry, I can't help you with that." This answer, and especially the period at the end of the sentence, is a dead-end from which you can easily wean your team members. Those who are service providers to people in other departments, if not also to actual clients, should not give this lame answer.

Answers like: "I see your point, let me look into it," or at least a logical explanation to the reasoning being the policy, works much better with the Real Knowledge approach. This will come to be spontaneously when you combine capability and a sense of influence with an inquisitive mind.

Real Knowledge: Test Yourself

- *When asked for advice or for an answer I do my best to give technique instead of knowledge.*

- *I focus on processes such as planning and make sure my employee evaluates alternatives first without connecting the process to the imagined results.*

- *It's more important for my employee to learn what I have to teach him than for me to teach him.*

- *Process-related ignorance on the part of my team members is used as an opportunity to deliver Real Knowledge techniques such as the three core skills and other principles (i.e. forgetting to alert me to a delay, etc.).*

- *Whenever I can, I delegate all decision making moments to my staff. I only make critical decisions.*

- *I am aware of the progress my team members are making in acquiring Real Knowledge: teaching them more skills, exposing them to more complex situations and propelling them gradually to professional independence.*

- *I make time to save time.*

- *If I feel resistance to using Real Knowledge techniques in training someone, I make sure it is not the result of my own insecurities.*

Part III

Simplicity Overview

Like in the case of other Kind Excellence skills, practicing Simplicity means exercising a new way of thinking. Part two is about the techniques that engage the mind in seeing as much of what is out there as possible and handling it in an effective way.

Simplicity is seeing what is real. It means understanding the origin of things, separating reality from perception, knowing ourselves, others, and as much of the world around us as possible. It's not acquiring knowledge that includes all these things, but rather the state of mind and the techniques that get us ready and actively willing to see.

In order to make practicing Simplicity easy I've integrated its principles under three powerful techniques:

- Seeing things as they truly are
- Locating cores—a core analysis technique
- Mastering Receptiveness

The first segment will improve our limited perception of reality by seeing things as they truly are and the ability to determine what is real and what is only perceived as real. Segment two is an excellent tool for identifying the origin of challenges and turning the process of resolving them into a focused effort. Finally, segment three will train you to control your ability to listen, digest information, and express yourself from a balanced place, so that you can really make the most out of Simplicity.

Each one of these segments is designed to increase human asset potential. Among its many benefits, Simplicity leads to innovation, effective feedback, saving time by narrowing in on the core, enhancing openness to criticism and different points of view, and conflict resolution. The secondary benefits of this segment are so significant that they alone have made it possible for me to convince managers to set aside their controlling patterns and start experimenting.

Let's go.

Chapter Five

Seeing Things as They Truly Are

Whatever authority I may have rests solely on knowing how little I know.
—Socrates

TO GET A FULL picture, managers have to listen to the whole truth. This includes things they do not want to hear and, without kindness and genuine encouragement, their staff would actually prefer to avoid bringing up. Seeing things as they truly are requires a certain humbleness and necessitates that the manager have enough self confidence to let go and actually see the whole truth.

Why Do We Not See Things as They Truly Are?

We have a subjective, and hence, skewed view of the world in our minds. The further away we are from what is real, the more prone we are to making the wrong decisions.

This bias has four leading causes:

- Socialization to answers rather than questions
- A limited capacity
- What we see is often not real
- Subjective representation

Socialization to Answers Rather Than Questions

Few people are capable of expressing with equanimity opinions that differ from the prejudices of their social environment. Most people are even incapable of forming such opinions.

—Albert Einstein

Once upon a time, people thought the earth was flat. They believed this with such conviction that any other idea seemed ridiculous. But they were wrong. Nowadays, realistic physicists acknowledge the phenomena of the universe as just that: perceived phenomena; they admit that the most accurate "findings" of sciences are often temporary "facts." They are serviceable and established until disproved.

It's Story Time (source unknown)

Think about a child, your son or daughter, or your nephew or your best friend's child. Imagine that last week, when they went to school, their teacher handed them a drawing of a rose and offered to let them paint it. The child reaches for blue (because that's her favorite color, of course), but the teacher quickly corrects her, "No darling, a rose is red; paint it red." This child just picks up red and paints the rose red. The same thing happens when the child wants to paint the leaves; leaves are green, right?

In no time at all, this child learns a valuable lesson: there is a "right" and a "wrong" way to doing things and the judge of "right" and "wrong" is someone else. She starts asking others what the world should be like. And if she does not find red nearby when she has a rose to color, she just sits and waits, doing nothing at all.

Thank you, Traci O'Neill, wherever you are, for sharing this and other anecdotes, and for doing your very best to raise a generation of creative and independent-minded children.

Unfortunately, most societies work very hard to create a sense that some people know what is real and what is not and establish that some things should just be a certain way.[*] This attempt at control seeps into thinking processes, and to the way we approach challenges. At some point, many of us start believing in things without questioning them.

As children we are taught that there are right answers and wrong answers, and that the adults know which are which. Most kids realize very early on that the path to success (and self fulfillment) involves pleasing adults rather than exercising an inquisitive mind. A child who asks too many questions and challenges adult assumptions is often considered difficult, or even completely undisciplined—just for asking questions! There is simply no time for that kind of disruptive behavior in the classroom!

Michael J. Gelb writes in his book *How to Think Like Leonardo Da Vinci*: "Although we all start life with a Da Vinci-like insatiable curiosity, most of us learned, once we got to school, that answers were more important than questions. In most cases, schooling does not develop curiosity, delight in ambiguity, and question asking skill. Rather, the thinking skill that is rewarded is figuring out the "right answer"—that is the answer held by the person in authority, the teacher."

Being in an answering mindset, rather than a questioning one, means we are more likely to re-use and apply our taught conclusions to a challenge rather than look at what is right in front of us. The result is a bunch of people who step into a situation seeing exactly what they are preprogrammed to see. Very few of your team members are going to express their own

---

[*] A basic illustration of this attempt is in behavioral patterns. With all the "Miss Manners" and other etiquette books, it is clear people believe practicing an established behavioral code gives a distinct edge.

opinions—most of them simply do not know what their opinions are because they have been trained to ignore them.

A Limited Capacity

The eye sees only what the mind is prepared to comprehend.
—Henri Bergson

I was lucky enough to spend five years of my life living and working in Berkeley, California. Though there are many aspects about Berkeley that stand out, it is the sun that I remember most. As the sun and shade highlighted different parts of the scenery every few minutes, every time I looked at the world I would notice different things. It was as if the sun was constantly re-focusing a high voltage spotlight on a certain house or hill.

Looking at this ongoing show the sun and the clouds were coordinating, I was often surprised to see new things I had never before seen. They were not new phenomena, and I must have seen them passing by every day, but I had never registered them.

You will find that this happens all the time with all of our senses. Our brain generalizes and reduces stimuli on an ongoing basis. We hear less, we see less, and we smell less than is truly there. Have you ever had someone comment on the fragrance of your aftershave or perfume when you cannot even smell it anymore?

While this selective mechanism is beneficial (I believe very few of us can keep their sanity without it), it is dysfunctional when it comes to understanding reality as a whole. That is because our conscious can only be aware of a fraction of reality at any given time.

Add to that the limitations of language. People that know five different names for five different shades of red can see five different shades of red. And, like Margaret Atwood says, the fact that "Eskimo have 52 names for snow," means they are sure to have a much more sophisticated perspective on what looks to most of us like white frozen water.

I'm sure you can see where this is leading us.

Let's spell it out. If we are not familiar with a certain concept, it is very likely that we will not notice it even in front of our noses. There's therefore no chance we would initiate an action based on that facet of a situation.

What We See Is Often Not Real

Everyone takes the limits of his own vision for the limits of the world.
—Arthur Schopenhauer

If it is not already enough that we only see a fraction of reality,* we actually distort reality by looking at it.

Anthropologists know that when they observe people they need to work very hard (and it is never perfect) to remove as much of their presence as possible. Their presence changes the behaviors they record (as the name "participant observation" indicates). The same is true for almost all human interaction. Do you know that employees change their behavior, even if ever so slightly, when you step into the room? Do you realize that any human dynamic changes once you add another member to the group?

Robert Fritz gives a beautiful example of this in his book, *The Path of Least Resistance*. "The artist and teacher Arthur Stern once took several of his students to Riverside Park in New York City. He pointed to three architectural structures across the

---

* Perception is only a part of it. Try actual physical limitation like not being able to see all the colors out there, or that we think substance is static while in fact particles are moving all over the place.

Hudson River: an apartment house, a storage tank, and a factory. Stern asked his students to name the color of the buildings. His students were in agreement that the apartments were red, the storage tank was white, and the factory was orange. Stern then handed the students some small gray cards, each with a small hole punched through it... the students were silent for quite a while, until one finally spoke. "They are all blue..."

Stern's students had discovered that what we see has a much higher likelihood to be something other than what is actually out there.

Subjective Representation

The universe is full of magical things, patiently waiting for our wits to grow sharper.
— *Eden Phillpotts*

Zen practitioners say that reality has its own existence outside of people's perception. They believe things have their own seed of truth and that the degree to which our senses and thinking processes are "clean" of previous impressions and knowledge, will determine how much of it we see. It is a matter of how close we can get, with our limited perceptions to seeing what is real. Zen monks spend years practicing a fresh perspective on things, trying to separate themselves and their preconceptions of the world, from what is right in front of them.

But most of us attach subjective meanings and information to things we see and hear, to the point that we can no longer differentiate between what is real and what we added in.

Thich Nhat Hanh, the Vietnamese Zen Buddhist monk (Nobel peace prize nominee 1967) puts it so beautifully in *The Sun My Heart*:

"Our mind creates categories—space and time, above and below, inside and outside, myself and others, cause and effect, birth and death, one and many, and puts all physical and psychological phenomena into categories like these before examining them and trying to find their true nature."

We let our own subjective interpretations, those that come from our own subconscious, take over what is truly there. We use subjective conclusions; the learning we acquired over years without verifying that our conclusions are justified. And yet these conclusions determine how we see the world.

We put people's appearances in categories. We quickly assign meaning to mannerisms and assume diction indicates intelligence. We even presume to know the feelings and intentions of others, all based on our subjective view of how things should be and what we think we know. We hardly ever bother to ask. And just as we apply those judgments to people, we use them when we look at the surrounding world.

While this is all understandable (seriously it would be impossible to have any conversation without making some assumptions), it is too widely used for our own good.

The "How-To" of Seeing Things as They Truly Are

This chapter offers a correcting mechanism. It focuses on all of the different stages of our misconceptions, thus providing internal and external guards to help buffer drawing faulty conclusions that stem from seeing only a segment of reality. As you go through the mechanisms, take note of their underlying aim to create a safe environment for sharing different perspectives. This is partly why this technique and the other techniques in this book work well with kindness, but do not benefit other management styles.

Be Aware of Your Own Limitations

Do you have any? Do you know them well enough to recognize them while they are at play?

Imagine for a moment that you could only see two dimensions instead of three. You would be looking at a ball thinking it's a circle, and for all you know the earth would seem like an infinite platform because you could walk on endlessly without ever reaching an end.* If you can only see a certain perspective of reality, you are likely to draw wrong conclusions.

Strip yourself of the assumptions you know. The fact is, you do not know what it is that you know. This realization will immediately put you in a questioning state of mind. That is if you can resist the intense, internalized habit developed through years of praise for correct answers instead of creative questions.

Once you've opened yourself up to beneficial doubt, a learned skill, go on to find your individual limitations, your general strengths, and weaknesses. We all have them. By knowing what you are great at and what other people can do better, and delegating tasks to those who can do them best, you save yourself time and increase your productivity.

Rediscovering your abilities, your strengths, and weaknesses can be a tricky process. Here are a few guidelines that can be used as discovery tools:

- Make a list of your tasks. Rate your own performances in each on a scale of 1–10. How well do you think you did?
- Consider how you would describe yourself, to yourself, if you were on a deserted island.
- What feedback do you keep getting from others?

---

* As in the beautiful *Flatland*, by Edwin A. Abbott.

- When working in a team, what are your leading contributions (i.e. planning, paying attention to detail, organizing, getting things done, integrating, etc.)?
- Of all the parts of your job which tasks do you like best, and which ones do you often try to avoid?

Now take into account hidden talents that you are unaware of, and weaknesses you resist acknowledging, and listen. If a comment comes up more than once, or if people fear your response, investigate it. If you are telling yourself you can't do something well enough, like market yourself to your supervisors, interview, or work through conflicts, try to see if you are insisting on generalizing a value like: "Those who advance do it by stepping on others" to prevent you from marketing, "If I turn someone down I'll hurt them, and hurting others is bad" stopping you from becoming a good interviewer, or work through conflicts. Values are great, but when generalized they could be hiding some great talents.

Knowing your own limitations also means finding out what you need to learn more about and what you should not bother to spend your time on. Though this book is not about team development, I cannot resist telling you that this technique is also one of the foundations for synergy. This is because if each one of your team members (yourself included) knows what they know and what they could improve on, then it is easy to tell who would be the best person for each project. It is the awareness of strengths and limitation that maximizes a team's potential because it enables the team to work with all of its available resources.

In my experience, when this awareness finds its way to the team, it is extremely easy to supervise and review the performances of team members. So much so that as an HR director my staff used to come to me, once tasks were assigned, asking me to supervise specific segments of the task because they knew it was not their strongest suit. What more can you ask for?

Understand Assumptions and How They Affect Behavior

It just so happens that our plans and actions are based on our conceptions and misconceptions. We all base our interactions with the world on basic assumptions, values, and other beliefs. These guide our conclusions, which in turn lead to actions. And actions that are based on our conceptions and misconceptions are not always effective. If our conclusion is off track, so will our actions be.

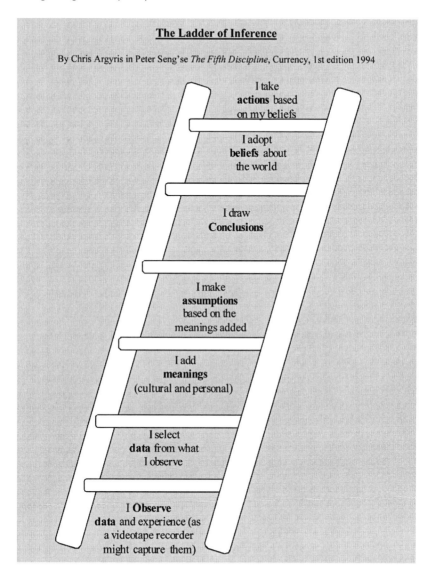

The Ladder of Inference

By Chris Argyris in Peter Seng'se *The Fifth Discipline*, Currency, 1st edition 1994

I take **actions** based on my beliefs

I adopt **beliefs** about the world

I draw **Conclusions**

I make **assumptions** based on the meanings added

I add **meanings** (cultural and personal)

I select **data** from what I observe

I **Observe** **data** and experience (as a videotape recorder might capture them)

When assumptions and misconceptions are directed toward people, Simplicity can save the day (and over time even prevent unnecessary emotional discomfort). Clarity can present itself once people start investigating and uncovering their basic assumptions.

Change the Focus of Things

This goes back to the beginning of this chapter. We can only be aware of so much at any given moment. In order to deal with a very complex reality we simplify things by creating categories, making assumptions, and reaching conclusions. This is good because you really cannot function, or even carry a simple conversation without it, but it gets in the way of seeing things.

Putting yourself at a different angle or highlighting things differently can help with seeing things you didn't notice before. Here are a few simple ideas to experience a change of focus:

- **Relocating the challenge**—Try to speculate about the solution of choice for your challenge. What if it were to happen in a different organization that you know well? Make sure the organization you choose is different than the one you are currently in. How would the organizational differences affect dealing with the challenge? Would the different culture change the communication around it? What can you learn from it?

- **Changing the direction of deduction**—Sketch the direction of dealing with your challenge from beginning to end and from end to beginning (if this is a project focus on your end goal and work backwards. Then switch the direction, start from what you think needs to be done, and lead it to the end goal). Review the differences between these two paths in terms of effectiveness and efficiency (reaching your goal, time, timing, energy, etc.).What causes the differences?

- **Using inner changes**—Look at your challenge (time permitting) at different times of day, different moods, and as you spend time with different people etc. Take note of the insights gained.

- **Exploring different perspectives**—Imagine what your clients would say, how your boss, team members, and employees would react. All of those are good sources for clues on what you may be missing.

Ask Other People's Opinions—Invite Disagreement

Solicit feedback and test your knowledge simply by asking people if your assumptions are correct. You can apply this (I'm avoiding the word *technique* as this should be a far more common approach to life, alas…) to interpersonal challenges as well as to understanding any other challenges.

As crazy as it may sound, you can actually ask your co-worker if the interpretation you have is true. You can check to see if you angered them or if they intended to hurt you by making a certain comment. And the same applies to any other assumptions we make when interacting with others.

And when it comes to other challenges, there is nothing like actively seeking different perspectives. It's kind of like changing the focus of things only you do not need to speculate. Ask people what could possibly go wrong with your plan or where you could be missing something.

Separate Packaging from Content

We are too impressed with packaging. We often use the way something is represented as an indication for what it is, and it's so powerful that it overrules the message. Why can't we just judge the message separately? I guess it comes from being efficient. If we had to look into everything, there would be no end to it. But we take this generalization too far.

Let's suppose a well-established lawyer wearing an expensive suit and a first-year graduate student wearing ratty sneakers are having an argument in your presence. Suppose the lawyer uses a very convincing tone of voice, while the student is less sure of himself. Not many people would actually spend the time to listen to the content of the discussion before assuming the lawyer is in the right.

While observation is an efficient mechanism, it is often misleading. Things are as they are regardless of who says them. We should evaluate observations with caution regardless of how they are being said. As Richard Feynman, who received a Nobel Prize in physics in 1965, and to me is the symbol of true genius, once said (referring to a disagreement he had with Einstein about Quantum Mechanics), "Nature doesn't care how smart you are, you can still be wrong."

I am not, obviously, recommending that you apply this principle to every little thing. But I find it quite useful when it comes to important decisions.

So there you have it. Seeing things as they truly are is already a skill you possess, and now it's time for Simplicity's second pillar—the core analysis technique.

Chapter Six

Locating Cores:
A Core Analysis Technique

R EMEMBER THE STONE AND the ripples analogy from chapter two? We compared the stone to a core action that propels secondary results—the ripples. And we reached two conclusions:

1. If you identify a core action leading to a chain of response actions that propel success, you want to invest time only in duplicating the core action. The response actions will occur as a by-product.
2. When faced with a dysfunction, it is vital to resolve its core and do it as close to its onset as possible. Investing time in resolving the chain of responses to that core is of very little use.

This segment of Simplicity takes a closer look into the technique that exposes core actions. It is a step by step tour of everywhere you need to go in the dialogue between your mind and reality to expose the causes of challenges and future desired results.

It is a subjective path which means it will lead you to the cores you believe cause reactions. I know, I've heard it before, you think it's worth very little if it's subjective. But I'm telling you, you're making up subjective theories and acting on them every day. The core analysis technique exposes your subjective conclusions to a reality test and to other people's opinions and conclusions. The hope is that by closing the gap, your perception will lead you to a better truth. You will have a focused, well defined, action plan that will lead to the results you desire and save you time and money along the way.

Shall we proceed then?

How Do You Go About Looking For a Core?

Training your team to look for cores demands a big change in thinking habits. This means you need to train them with all the ammunition Real Knowledge can provide. Remember to highlight opportunities to use the core analysis technique, but more importantly remember to do it yourself. Your personal example of asking core questions will provide your staff with the strongest change incentive.

Though this section is written as training for you, the first thing you need to do once you have mastered it, is to turn and start training your employees to use it.

How then do you go about looking for a core?

You do the simplest thing you can think of—just ask *why*. Ask why about things that seem obvious to everyone. It never ceases to amaze me how people tend to just accept a situation which makes no sense without questioning it, simply because it was in place when they arrived. Whole organizations practice policies that make no sense without a single employee raising their hand to ask why. Start asking why things are so. Do not stop digging until you find the core reasons.

"Dropping in a core" can create change in two directions: resolving an existing challenge and planning for a successful change implementation. The core analysis technique below applies to both situations:

- **Resolving an existing challenge**—such as a conflict, dysfunctional behavior, lack of trust in the team, or high turnover. Here, core analysis is used by backtracking from the ripples to the core.
- **Planning a successful application process for a change that is about to take place**—such as a preparation for a new project, increasing motivation, planning an effective training, getting ready for an upcoming review or even a foreseen merge, locating the core that will lead to best results effectively and with the least amount of effort. Here, core analysis is used by "dropping" the core into the situation leading to desired results.

Though the situations are different in both cases, the core analysis technique stays the same. The application is in fast-forward for one and in rewind for the other; however, that is only a chronological aspect, and the process of identifying the core stays the same.

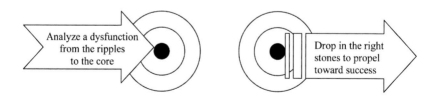

In both cases you start by looking at the ripples, which are the secondary responses that either exist or that you are striving to achieve. You go backward until you identify the core actions that have caused the problem, or the ones that will promote your purpose.

Basically, you look at each secondary result and trace back things to their origin by discovering why they occurred. You will know when you hit a core because there is not a deeper level that can explain why the secondary response exists and investigating further isn't going to provide any new input.

If you can answer your "why" question, or have others help you find the answer, ask why again, until you feel you have reached a dead end. Test it until you're sure, and when you are, you're there.

Let's start asking some why questions when looking at the organizational level in the following example:

- o "Why do we let marketing change the specifications of the product without changing the delivery date for the product?"
- o "Because we need to stay competitive and if we change the delivery date the client might prefer to go to one of our competitors next time."

Now, *that* makes sense. So can we stop investigating further?

Yes, it makes sense, but stopping now is too early. Just because something makes sense does not make it a core. You can do very little to promote your organization with such an understanding.

As we start separating cores from their secondary results, let's try this—ask "why" again!

"Why would changing our delivery date mean the risk of losing the client?" An answer such as "it's a tough market" is not going to get you far. Maybe you do not devote enough time to creating a clear contract with your client at the beginning of the project letting them know that changes in requirements or product specifications will affect the production date. Or maybe your marketing department is out of touch with the development department. Or maybe the development department needs to improve the ongoing communication channels with your client and its marketing division.

These are not yet cores, but can you feel how much more can be done about changing things already?

Moving from the organizational level inward, let's look at dysfunction in a team:

○ "Why do our meetings feel like a waste of time? It just seems like we talk and talk and yet nothing really changes."

○ "Because no one runs the meetings, there is no agenda, and there is no follow-up from last time."

Hold it right there. Look closely. Do not be tempted to think it's time to stop asking why. Not having anyone run the meetings, having no agenda, or follow-up are not cores. They are good reasons for complaint, but if you change them you are bound to hit the resistance of their causes. Try to start having someone run the meetings, or to have an agenda—even sending it to everyone before the meeting, and ask for a progress report after the meeting. Things may change for a week or two but you will soon discover that no substantial change has been made. The cores that are leading to these complaints will regain power in no time.

Then ask "why" again:

"Why don't we have anyone run the meetings, prepare an agenda, or follow up?"

Again there can be countless answers and only you can know which they are, but here are a few common causes:

- Staff meetings are considered time away from work, and the less time devoted to talking the more work gets done.
- The team avoids hitting the real issues in order to maintain the status quo.
- Team members are not informed enough to be involved in strategizing, hence meetings are limited to general impractical talk.

And suppose you believe the real reason that meetings proceed in this manner is for none of these reasons. Suppose you think that it has to do with a specific team member that manipulates the conversation, leaving very little chance for others to participate. You would just go on asking why until you reach the core. We'll return to this example shortly, but first let's take a look at the technique.

There are eight steps to detecting a core:

1. Identify causes and secondary results.
2. Set secondary results as the outer circle.
3. Target secondary results and ask why.
4. Establish the answer of the results investigation as a one circle in.
5. Look at causes and ask why (again and again until you can't take it anymore) in response to the circle you've just established.
6. Start from the core and make sure you've covered all the secondary results.

7. If you haven't covered all secondary results go back to step one and look for another core.

8. You're there, but wait… Test it.

Remember the core analysis technique before you is not going to lead you to the right objective answer (as if there really is one). It's not a magic trick. What it will do is lead you to the core actions you need to apply according to your and your team's own understanding of the world. Once you have that, you can run it by other experts, and since most managers do not do either, you are well ahead of the game.

Let's look at our team meeting example from before and take it through the technique:

Step 1—Identify causes and secondary results

Our first response is that meetings feel like a waste of time.

Ask yourself: is that a cause or a secondary result? Naturally, meetings are a waste of time for a reason. They do not have to be a waste of time but something is turning them into a waste of time. That something is a cause and if a statement has a cause it is clearly a secondary result.

Step 2— Set secondary results as the outer circle

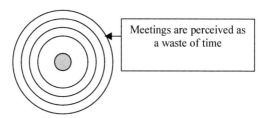

Meetings are perceived as a waste of time

Step 3—Target secondary results and ask why

"Why is it that our meetings feel like a waste of time? It just seems like we talk and talk and yet nothing really changes?"

Step 4—Establish the answer of the results investigation as a one circle down

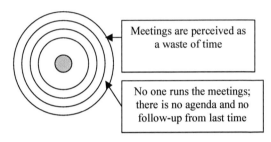

Meetings are perceived as a waste of time

No one runs the meetings; there is no agenda and no follow-up from last time

Step 5—Look at the cause and ask why in response to the circle you've just established

"Why don't we have anyone run the meetings, prepare an agenda, or follow up?"

Once you establish the answer, place it at the next inner circle until you feel you can't ask why anymore.

Core analysis questions are, by definition, core directed. This means they focus on one thing and one thing alone; finding the fundamental reasons for the existence of the challenge. This goes back to starting from the end—if you know where you are going you can save everyone time and effort. Hence, core analysis questions do not bother about some questions. They focus solely on the essentials for effectively resolving the challenge at hand.

You are a manager in a large telecommunication company. In your weekly staff meeting you realize there have been three incidences this week of angry customers complaining that their account was overcharged. Trying to get to the bottom of this, you ask your team some questions:

Kind Excellence Questions	Other
What does the process of handling accounts include?	How did you answer these clients?
Where are the main differences between the model and how it's practiced?	What past interactions led to this situation?
Where can things go wrong?	How does it manifest itself every day?
Why are they going wrong?	Where in the organizational structure is it coming from?
What is causing them to go wrong?	Was whatever was missing taught during training weeks?
Why?	Is this response given to certain representatives?
Why?	Can we offer these clients something to make them feel happy?
Why?	And other questions in many different directions.

Core analysis questions are focused, steadily going from peripheral to the heart of the matter. The other approach asks specific, yet scattered questions. While other approaches seem to go over the whole spectrum of possible issues, core questions lead directly to where action is required—and only there. It's a step-by-step approach to investigating the core causes of challenges. Without it, you pretty much have to check everything that can be causing it until you hit what you think is causing it, and test it until something works.

Step 6—Start from the core and make sure you've covered all the secondary results.

Now go backward and see if it all makes sense to you. If you think the cause might be this one team member who manipulates the conversation, and after wondering why this is going on, you discover that this team member has unrealistic expectations as to their role in the group, go back and check it. Is this the only cause? Can this really explain the entire problem?

If this person is causing the problem then you've got a single core analysis and you can continue. If he or she is not the only cause, you will need to repeat this process to identify the other cores involved.

Step 7—If you haven't covered all secondary results, go back to step one and look for another core.

Step 8—Test it.

If you find your staff, your co-workers, supervisors, and anyone else you can run this by (including customers, if the challenge is appropriate) to be in general agreement, you are probably on to something. If not, it's time to reassess your assumptions and go back to the drawing board.

Testing a theory often leads to redefining the challenge itself. People will tell you, "Wait, but you know what is also troubling… " Stay open to those comments. You might just discover that though meetings are perceived as a waste of time, people actually want to have great meetings and they even know how to achieve them. But the problem is they are too overwhelmed with unrealistic production expectations that leave them no time to spare. Be flexible and listen. It's in your best interests.

Testing is vital because, often, after you devote time to perusing an idea you start getting attached to it. You start convincing yourself that you are right and everything that does not seem to fall into place kind of evaporates in order to allow for your conclusions. So stay open to these feedbacks. Like any feedback, it can be used to keep you away from making mistakes and wasting your time.

But hang on a minute, didn't I say that cores are used to both solve problems and create desired results? All I've been talking about so far was problems. What about propelling a successful change application?

When it comes to human asset management trying to achieve long-lasting results in preparing for a change, in training, or in any other human asset, desired results require multiple core analyses. Actually, trying to lead teams to outstanding results requires three core skills. And you know the secret recipe—or at least you will know it when you are done reading this book. The interesting thing is that it's always Real Knowledge, Simplicity, and Systemic Thinking—no matter what result you are trying to create. Kind Excellence techniques work for preparing for a big change such as a merger, just as much as they work for an everyday challenge such as giving feedback. It's these three core skills that form an effective interview, build intrinsic motivation, and on and on.

The core analysis technique is very easy to apply, and with seeing things as they truly are, you've almost got Simplicity ready to go. The third member of Simplicity's group is next. I'm sure you will find it as simple and powerful as the first two.

Chapter Seven

Receptiveness

One of the advantages of being disorderly is that one is constantly making exciting discoveries.

—A. A. Milne

RECEPTIVENESS IS A STATE of mind; an empty one. Since Benjamin Hoff's book *The Tao of Pooh*, Winnie the Pooh has become my western Taoist hero. Consider the mood Pooh is constantly in. It's this state of being happy and excited yet not overworked. Pooh treats mishaps as the best thing that could possibly happen and the worse you will hear him say if something turns out not quite how he expected is a faint, "Oh bother." His mood is an even plateau most of the time.

Well, that's Pooh, and I hardly expect you to start practicing Taoism; however, you can benefit a great deal from understanding how the guiding principles of both work. If you know how to use this Winnie the Pooh mind set at will, there is a lot in it for you and your team.

I always find it a bit amusing and somewhat frustrating when training materials give instructions like, "Listen with an open mind," or "Have no desire to protect yourself." But they neglect to provide an understanding of exactly how I'm supposed to shut down my emotions and empty my mind. And since that's what Receptiveness is all about we have to venture, for the fourth time, on a Real Knowledge quest.

Much like the core analysis technique, Receptiveness requires your personal example along with a training effort of others. Just like in the previous chapter I will be referring to your own training, but notice that once you get infected with the Receptiveness bug you can use the same technique to get your employees on board.

This chapter will help you take control of the mode your mind is in. In doing so, you can start using your state of mind to your benefit by gradually taking hold of the reins of your intellect and emotions. Now you are leading them instead of them leading you. By the end of this chapter you should be well acquainted with the different tools that are at your disposal to achieve Receptiveness. But be warned, Receptiveness is the hardest Kind Excellence technique to master.

It's ironic that freeing our mind of thoughts and emotions would be so difficult to accomplish since it's such a passive act. It's difficult because, as you will discover when you start to practice it, it's really intrusive. If you are to reach a balanced place of listening, processing, and responding, you first need to be aware of the thoughts and emotions that stand in your way. And that's no easy task.

Do you think you can do it? Are you ready to expose yourself to the dysfunctional elements of your own thinking processes? Are you willing to practice letting go of ineffective thinking patterns that you have gotten used to?

If you are, these are valuable benefits in their own right. I could tell you how priceless it is to even just be aware of your own thinking glitches (what professionals call "heuristics"), but it doesn't stop there. The real reward will be reflected in the performance of your team; after all, our goal is to maximize their potential, not yours. Receptiveness leads to positive reactions to new ideas and changes, characterized by exploration, future orientation, and persistence to resolve challenges. Getting your team to practice Receptiveness will directly enhance skills like customer service, sales, development, and marketing. After all, listening and knowing how to communicate is golden. Top that with a high tolerance for ambiguity, trust, closeness, and intrinsic motivation, and I'm sure you will be eager to start practicing it tomorrow.

The "How-To" of Receptiveness

Receptiveness is the ability to control your mindset and bring it as close as you can to a place of emptiness, free of emotions, conclusions, and expectations, at will. Reaching this state is valuable when you listen, process your thoughts, and respond. I'll show you that you can recognize the "noises" in your thinking (which result in emotional reactions) and gradually eliminate them to provide a "cleaner" form of processing.

Unless you are a monk, a martial arts specialist, or otherwise trained to use Receptiveness in your day-to-day life, it is unlikely you will be able to instantly move into a place of mental and emotional balance when you need to. But by gradually practicing Receptivencss you can learn to shorten the time it takes you to find that state of mind and jump into it. So you will probably still get defensive, offended, or even excited to the point it impedes your ability to be receptive, but you will learn to recognize this and reinforce Receptiveness quickly thereafter.

With sufficient practice, you will be able to achieve Receptiveness by creating a temporary distance between yourself and your thoughts and emotions. It's kind of like you get to watch a movie about how you are acting and feeling a few seconds before you have to choose your response.

Many managers find it surprising that people can be thrown off balance by extreme positive emotions just as much as negative emotions. You are just as much at risk of missing an important point when you are excited your team won, as you are when frustrated by a team loss.

Some people do well in adjusting to Receptiveness. Others find it easy to be their own observers when it comes to emotions, but completely lose balance when it comes to ideas they believe in. Or they may be cool and relaxed when positive things happen and overworked when something goes wrong. You need to discover yourself, the areas in which you can step aside and respond from a more balanced place, and the times when you are too involved to bother.

We all feel most comfortable with ideas and concepts we already know or believe in. Receptiveness means that you let yourself be exposed to anything except what you already believe in and know. You notice it, you can observe how it affects your emotions, you realize what conclusions you draw from it, and during this whole time you are positioned outside of the experience. It's a clear detachment that allows you to be more objective.

Initially you should not judge your performances (and those of others) by results, but rather master the techniques first. It is very rare for anyone to master Receptiveness in two weeks, just like it's unusual for a student to wrap their mind around chess strategies in two weeks. It all comes down to how often you practice and how dedicated you are to mastering the techniques. (I'm still working on it... I've gotten so much better though.)

Receptiveness can be used in four different communication stages:

- **Evaluate** your state of Receptiveness
- **Meditate** with your eyes open
- **Test It**—Check to see if you understand things correctly
- **Respond** (when a Receptive response is required)

Step #1: Evaluate—Can You Be Receptive in the Moment?

If your answer is no, reschedule and get back to that person or the issue at hand when you are ready. You can say something like, "You know I really want to hear what you have to say, but I feel I can't listen the way I'd like to right now. Let's schedule a time now to talk later." This goes back to recognizing our limitations and responding to them.

In order to practice Receptiveness you have to be what psychologists would call, "congruent." Basically this means you will need to be in touch with your own feelings and let others know where you are. You could be angry with this person, have just received wonderful news, or simply be in a hurry. Any one of these reasons should be enough to postpone a conversation if it affects your emotional balance.

Just be sure to follow up and re-schedule at a better time.

Step #2—Meditate with Your Eyes Open*

Meditation is a state in which you focus on a word, a spot, or any other focal point, to gently clear the mind of all the rest. It is a highly focused state that is directed inward. It's obviously the best way to understand Receptiveness because during a meditative mode one practices freeing the mind from all thoughts and emotions and regains a place of emotional balance. Getting into a meditative mode is a process that gets easier with time. Hence, people who practice meditation regularly can effortlessly switch back and forth from detachment to being present in a matter of seconds.

The power of meditation can be best understood by its application to martial arts. In Kung Fu, for example, this meditative-focused ability allows the practitioner to draw back, observe, and then enhance the attacker's direction. Thus, allowing the attacker to fall with their own energy, instead of applying resistance.

"For example, if a punch is thrown at chest level, the defender might fluidly turn 90 degrees to avert the blow while adding an additional push or pull, 'helping' the attacker to proceed in the direction he or she was already heading," wrote Charles Manz in *Emotional Discipline.*

A person practicing meditation techniques can observe messages and other people and, because she is not emotionally and intellectually bound to anything, can easily see the best way to direct their energy. This means that by practicing Receptiveness a manager can more easily direct an employee's emotions, challenging messages, or other inputs directed at him, to their most effective resolution without personally getting entangled.

---

* There are many different kinds of meditation. I am only referring to the kind that isn't for religious or directional purposes (without a goal presented as an image to achieve).

I am always surprised to see how many managers have used some form of meditation at one point or another. If you have used meditation before, all you have to do is transform that same ability to everyday life and practice it with your eyes open. If you haven't, give me your hand, and I'll take you there.

I have no intention of training you to meditate. I am going to present you with the relevant core techniques that stem from meditation:

- Filtering your thoughts
- Balancing your emotional gauge

Filtering Your Thoughts

Managers who participate in communication workshops sometimes confuse Receptiveness with different listening models.* Obviously, the listening aspects of Receptiveness are widely used in areas such as therapy, counseling, and anthropological research; however, there is more to Receptiveness than listening.

Receptiveness also consists of how you process new information in your mind, regardless of any interaction, and how you choose to respond.

I am telling you to free your mind of thoughts, but how does one go about actually accomplishing it?

Freeing your mind of thoughts, ideas, and conclusions is a process that takes time. You want to empty your mind, but

---

* Communication experts define many kinds of listening that would fall into this category including active listening, dialogic listening, passive listening, and many other professional terms. I'm not going to go into the specifics as each of these involve an enormous amount of specific knowledge, and we don't have time for it all. Instead I would like to focus on the core skills required in order to achieve these different types of listening and more.

thoughts keep jumping in. You are listening to your employee, but thoughts of the meeting tomorrow with the CEO keep creeping into your mind. So you tell yourself, "No, I'm going to focus on what he is saying." And suddenly, the efforts to eliminate other messages are becoming an interruption. Instead of thinking about the meeting, you are constantly interrupted by efforts to eliminate those thoughts. By trying to rid the thoughts that interrupt focus, you are creating a new interruption. So what should you do?

During meditation you focus on your breath, one particular sound, or a repetitive mantra. In this situation your focus is the content at hand. Whenever other thoughts come in, gently indicate to yourself they do not belong in your mind at this moment. It's a short mental note every now and again, not a constant effort. It's meant to be a natural process that has a place and a time, not a crusade to succeed right away. Like any other Real Knowledge technique, with enough practice, you will find fewer interruptions over time.

You can also try to redirect your wandering thoughts. Focus on the speaker and extend the time you focus on their message by thinking of questions that will elaborate and clarify their point of view. Replace the, "What can I do for this person?" with, "How does this person see themselves and their situation?"

Receptiveness is a Real Knowledge technique. The more you practice it the faster you will acquire it. The good news is that as a Real Knowledge technique, you can practice Receptiveness on simple challenges. There is really no need to limit yourself to situations in which you are emotionally invested. Starting with little challenges will have the same training quality as applying the technique to emotionally charged situations.

Enhance your abilities when you're not interacting with others by paying attention to the first responses you have to new things.

What are your initial thoughts? Can you delay your response and keep an empty mind for the first 10 seconds that you come across a new message? How about 20 seconds? Do not attempt to overcome your thoughts or change them. Simply point out to yourself that each such new input is an opportunity for you to practice Receptiveness.

Think about it this way: If you were asked to repeat what your employee just said, how well would you do?

Calibrating Your Emotional Gauge

A receptive mode is a physically and emotionally balanced state. In regards to Receptiveness any extreme emotion means being off balance. This includes feelings like frustration, anger, and impatience. But it also includes exhilaration and excitement. The feelings that describe emotional balance best are self-confidence and calmness. Imbalance is associated with tension (be it positive or negative in nature), while balance feels neutral.

Luckily, our emotions are found to be strongly connected to our bodies and minds. So, though at this point in time we do not know how to take control of our emotions, and I for one would regret the day we do, we can trigger in to the physical and mental signs we have in order to recognize our emotional state and apply the appropriate actions.

In her book *Change Your Questions Change Your Life,* Marilee Adams, Ph.D. uncovers the process that leads to emotions; in a split second we respond to new, usually conflicting input by asking ourselves a question. The answer to that question leads to an emotional reaction, which is followed by a physical reaction. With a little practice, we can recognize the physical response instantly, and use it as an indication for our emotions.*

In other words, our thoughts determine how we feel.

Consider the difference in your response to the same situation under two different assumptions; your colleague commented that you should consider changing your approach to solving a certain problem while your boss was in the room. How would you feel or respond if you thought:

- Your co-worker has hidden motivations to make you look less impressive to your boss, perhaps, to highlight how much more superior he wants to be perceived.
- Your colleague has your best interests in mind and is truly concerned.

It's the assumptions you make that will determine your emotional reaction. To a great extent, our thoughts control our emotions. The problem begins when we do not recognize that we are responding emotionally to an issue. In fact, sometimes the more emotionally invested we are in a situation the higher the likelihood that our mind will not recognize that we are emotional.

An emotional response immediately triggers a physical reaction. So though we may not be in touch with our emotional reaction, we can easily recognize physical reactions. I always treat emotional imbalance as a riddle waiting to be solved. You have the physical reaction, once you identify it, you can link it to a statement, revise the statement and bang—you're balanced.

All it takes is practicing introspection. A good place to practice

---

* This idea isn't new. Check out *Your Erroneous Zones* by Wayne W. Dyer for a comprehensive understanding of this mind-body-feelings connection and how to use it to your benefit.

Real Knowledge is by exploring simple cases. Next time you are exposed to a message that conflicts with your expectations, (preferably something you read or heard outside of a direct conversation), pay attention to your physical signs. Is your body shrinking a bit? Do you feel your heartbeat accelerating, sweat on your hands, your fingers fretting, or maybe you feel numb, as if you can't focus?

What Can Kind Excellence Skills Do for You? A Success Story

When managers get trained to use Kind Excellence skills they normally go through a three-month training plan. First they spend six hours to get acquainted with the skills. Then they get one-on-one training to learn how to apply the skills to their everyday lives.

This was the third session I had been working with a manager one-on-one, and though he understood the skills, we made very little progress. The issues were on the table, we kept making plans to change things, only to discover a week later that there was no change. We both agreed there was something deeper that was getting in our way. In other words, it was not a lack of understanding the change required that was holding him back—it was a resistance to change in the first place.

Once we established this simple understanding we started practicing Receptiveness separately from the challenge at hand. I did not question progress on the goals of the project. At this stage, all I cared about was mastering the technique. I did not ask him to change. I made it clear where change was needed. In three weeks the manager reported that he was done. Now he wanted to apply the skills to a different challenge. One of his employees was resisting feedback and blocking every possibility of change or progress.

Guess what? This manager no longer needed my help. He had the answer already. All I had to do was review how I did it with him.

"Your body and mood send you a message long before your mind does. You just need to learn your body language, think of it as your very own, built in warning system," writes Adams in *Change Your Questions Change Your Life.*

Now expand your awareness to more complex situations and different emotions including, feeling smug, overly excited, and other such responses. All you need to do is use this physical reaction as a signal, a light bulb flashing in your brain. Once you notice your physical signs check which thought is triggering it and change it.

Are you criticizing yourself? Are you telling yourself how extremely superior you are in this moment of success? Can you feel the tension—positive or negative that accompanies these statements? These sentences that, in all likelihood, stem from some insecurity (yes, we all have them) are the source of your imbalance.

Be aware of what you say to yourself, and let go. Your sophisticated human machine will naturally take care of the rest for you; just practice, sit back, and enjoy. Do not force it. Let repetition do the job for you.

Got it?

Good.

Now train your team members to use it.

With your employees' agreement you can improve their ability to gain balance. You can observe their physical reactions and, if you all agree, a certain physical sign can serve as a hint which you can take part in highlighting. You want to notice how their physical reactions change when not in emotional balance. Do they vary their rhythm of speech? Does their body language give them away?

Be very gentle because this is a very intrusive type of feedback.

Keep in mind that until you master Receptiveness, listening will not feel like it did before. Suddenly your mind will start engaging in inner talk. It will be comparing what was objectively said and the input your mind has been adding to it. You'll start observing your responses. That's okay. You are practicing a new technique and just like you would have thoughts jumping in when you were learning to meditate, you will have reactions when you try to listen. By accepting them, and noticing what's going on, things will change over time. If you get too angry or frustrated during a conversation, interrupt it, and get back to it later when you can regain your balance. If you've agreed to accept a message when you were not in your balance zone, go back and correct it. All it takes is being aware.

Step #3—Test It

All truths are easy to understand once they are discovered, the point is to discover them.

—*Galileo*

Let's say you're having a conversation. You think you have mastered Receptiveness, and you're really listening to messages objectively. This step is designed to put it to the test and give you pointers for improvement, if needed.

If, as you believe, you have mastered Receptiveness then you will find it very easy to understand the logic of a contradiction or a new message.

Next time you come across something you initially disagree with, put this hypothesis to the test. You do not need to agree with the message. You only need to understand its logic.

It's Story Time
Honey, what's for Dinner? (source unknown)

A husband, troubled by his wife's hearing loss, thought it might be time to get her a hearing device. He was not sure how to convey this message gently, so he called the family's physician for advice. The doctor sent him off with a simple test he could do at home to evaluate his wife's hearing loss.

"What you need to do is stand 20 feet from her and tell her something in a regular voice to see if she can hear you. If she doesn't respond, gradually repeat what you were saying and get closer until she does."

That same night, while the husband was reading a book in his study and his wife was preparing dinner in the kitchen, he decided to try the doctor's advice. In a regular voice he asked, "Honey, what's for dinner?" No response.

He got up from his chair and came within 15 feet of his wife, "Honey, what's for dinner?" Again, he received no response. Now, already within the same room as his wife he asked again, but still there was no reply. Finally, he stepped behind her and asked the question louder than before, "HONEY, WHAT'S FOR DINNER?"

"Bob, for the fourth time, we're having roast beef!"

Once you're ready, and you think you understand the message, repeat it and ask, "Is that correct?"

Remember, what someone says and what we hear can be very different. We all have our personal assumptions, values, and beliefs that can actually distort what is really being said.

If the source of the message believes you have understood the message, and the logic behind it in full, then you've passed the test. If they do not you might need to go back and practice some more.

Step #4—A Receptive Response

As I mentioned earlier, Receptiveness is not limited to how you listen and process things in your mind. The great importance of Receptiveness is also how you respond.

One of the best places to look for how to respond in a receptive mode is in couples' counseling. Since conflicts between couples are probably one of the most emotionally loaded interactions, and since we have a strong motivation to resolve these conflicts, it's a perfect place to draw on for tools.

According to the Imago approach (step 3 and step 4 are heavily influenced by Imago approach techniques), a couples' therapy methodology developed by Harville Hendrix, Ph.D. and his wife Helen LaKelly Hunt, Ph.D., this would be a good time to ask if there is more information the speaker wants to share. Acknowledge their logic and emotions. Ask if you can respond. I encourage managers to try this. But these days, since business does not always go well with emotions, it is not a must.

Now that you have openly absorbed the information another person has presented, and you did it from a place of emotional balance and with your mind open, you are almost ready to respond.

You've done so well this far. We're almost there, so hang on and do not drop Receptiveness yet!

Many wonderful listeners fall into this trap. They postpone their response, hold their breath, and let the other person talk. And, once it's their turn, they let go of the leash and all their emotions start flying through the air. That kind of a response is a good indication you have not been in a receptive mode.

You are invited back into the theater, which is screening your own movie. Can you see what you feel and think? Can you keep a distance from it enough to respond in a Taoist, Winnie-the-Pooh–like way? If not, and the topic is of importance to you or to the other person, take a break and get back into the discussion when you're ready. Go back and re-read the meditation skills we covered earlier.

Receptiveness and Boundaries

While all this openness, listening, and attentiveness are going on, the question of boundaries is in close proximity. Why? Because when you open a door people need to understand where the hinges are, otherwise, in an attempt to make way for their own interests, they'll walk all over it. In the absence of clear boundaries, people test the world around them to see how they fit in.

This may feel like two opposite powers working against each other; on the one hand being in tune with other's wants and needs and on the other hand keeping your own. While wearing a receptive hat, managers may be at risk of losing control, right?

Wrong.

Would it surprise you to learn that the number-one skill I work on with managers who suffer from "boundaries invasion" is Receptiveness?

Receptiveness works for listening, but it is also a powerful self-listening tool. Kindness cannot exist if you are not kind to yourself first. And the truth of the matter is, the two can co-exist. Being receptive does not mean you have to agree all the time or avoid conflicts. It just defines how you choose to listen and express your response.

I find that managers allow their employees to cross their boundaries for three reasons:

- Trying to avoid conflicts.
- Thinking that their expectations are obvious and expecting others to just understand them. This leads to a cycle of crossed boundaries and constant disappointment in others.
- They haven't formed their expectations.

These issues do not stem from Receptiveness. In fact, these all come from not expressing expectations in the first place. Receptiveness creates this aspect of communication. It can dissolve a fear of conflicts by providing managers with conflict resolution skills. Receptiveness will help managers tune in with their own expectations and express their expectations to others.

Managers think that if they allow themselves to get personal, open, and friendly with their staff, the ability to practice their authority in times of need will be diminished. Just like with kindness and with management success, this is a false link. It's the skills we're missing which is the cause, not Receptiveness. We think that if we eliminate being kind and receptive it will enhance authority; however, communicating our expectations to begin with will get far better results!

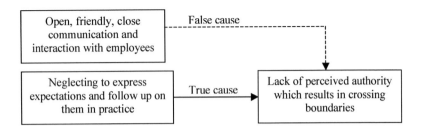

Begin by defining your expectations. Most managers need their staff to inform them of progress that is unsatisfactory in respect to scheduled deadlines (those should be agreed upon together), to bring up areas of concern immediately, to make an effort to promote projects themselves, and to make progress in agreed areas that require personal improvement. Managers expect honesty, and for their staff to try to be the best they can be. If you have other expectations, write them down and express them.

It wouldn't hurt to talk about expectations as mutual territory that can adjust over time. Once agreed upon, it's your employees' responsibility to try and work with your expectations; however, it's your job to share it with them. It's valuable information that can speed up everyone's ability to work together.

Being in a receptive mode doesn't mean you need to agree or do what others want. It only means you need to stay open to new messages and deliver messages from a balanced place. Look for a solution that can work for all, but do not give up what you want and need, or the organizational goals.

Managers are often uncomfortable by Receptiveness. Over the years I discovered that there is a legitimate fear behind these responses. They lack skills to support control as they let go of their "I'm in charge" position. That's where Kind Excellence skills make a huge difference. You will get a chance to practice them next.

It's Story Time
Once Upon a Time

As a lieutenant in the Israeli Army I had two soldiers under my command. These privates were providing professional duties such as running psychological surveys. But as they were part of the military, I was also responsible for their personal lives in the unit, scheduling leaves, attending to their health when they were sick, etc. I established a very informal interaction with them, avoiding the distance many officers choose to keep in order to obtain command. We worked in a friendly environment; I asked and they followed.

One day the base we were serving on had a 24-hour closure for security reasons. To my surprise one of the privates declared she was planning to go out anyway. "Who's going to know?" she asked. That was a slap in my face. "I'll know, and you're not going anywhere," was my reply. She simply dismissed my authority. I was too shocked to reply so I asked her, very firmly, to leave the office and come back in ten minutes. I needed time to think about how I would react.

I was upset. It was clear to see that my friendly approach was at fault. When she returned I explained to her how severely incorrect I thought her actions were and that I expected her to choose an appropriate punishment for her behavior.

"But you are my friend," she said. "How can you be so close to us all the time and suddenly turn into our commander?" And then it hit me. "I am your commander. If you want your commander to treat you like a friend, it's up to you to understand the boundaries of our relationship," I replied. I was 21 and I had a lot to learn.

I never gave up on a receptive approach to my soldiers or the employees that worked for me later. But I realized very quickly that though it's their job to understand the boundaries, it is my place to explain my expectations up front. Receptiveness needs to be coupled with clear expectations; the two are potentially contradicting elements that complement each other.

Chapter Eight

Practice Simplicity

Simplicity—Try It Out

THE CASE STUDY IN this chapter is designed to show you how simplicity applies to practice. I chose a somewhat extreme situation at a departmental level for emphasis. In real life, Simplicity skills can and should be used for small, simple, and everyday challenges. Core analysis technique should be used for thinking about any challenge you want to resolve or any future outcome you are trying create. Receptiveness and seeing things as they truly are should be used everyday, not just when you're meeting for an annual review. And all should be modeled by your personal example and taught to your staff as new skills.

You will benefit from this exercise most if you try and answer it yourself by using Simplicity (and Real Knowledge too if you wish) before you look at my lead. You can do it!

Okay, let's see what we've got here.

There Is Nothing Like Experience
A Case Study Report

A Medical Systems Company
Leading manufacturing department

Frustration, conflict, and distrust in management were all threatening to make this team of experts fall apart. The new, inexperienced manager, knowing intuitively that he was entering a lose-lose situation was pressured to accept consulting assistance. How was he going to regain the trust of his new team without going against management? How would he ever patch the gap of distrust in time to avoid losing the department's experts that were highly expensive to replace? And how should he position himself in respect to his staff?

The Facts:
- *High levels of tension were being experienced by employees.*

- *Power struggles, as well as interpersonal rivalries were present in the team. New employees felt uncomfortable asking questions and the team was divided into self-interest groups.*

- *A new competitive incentive plan was implemented.*

- *The incentive plan encouraged performance-based deception, which now dominated the relationship with management, thus reducing productivity and increasing destructive behavior when management wasn't around.*

- *Three managers had come and gone within a year. At one point, one of the senior professional team members had been promoted to a management position and was later replaced by an outside recruit.*

- *Team size had grown from 5 to 21 employees over a period of 3 months.*

The best place to begin is from the end. What does this manager need as his end result?

- To overcome negative emotions without getting stuck in the middle.
- To reinstate a committed staff that intends to stay.

Most consultants I know neglect to identify the core. In past years I would have recommended a dynamic workshop to rebuild trust and remove the new incentive plan. I would have also tried to look into the reasons for the many changes that had occurred in such a short amount of time and talked long and hard to management to avoid creating more changes in the near future.

It sounded so good I had almost convinced myself that it would surely work.

Only I doubt that it would.

There are deep reasons for this distrust. It comes from outside the team. Even if the new manager, through hard work, could bring the team back together, it would have to be by going against management values. He would have to say "we… and they" if he was to gain the trust of the team.

And who is to say that removing the incentive plan, which seemed to be the direct cause for deceptive performances, would have made any difference. It's like saying that the First World War would not have erupted if Franz Ferdinand, the heir to the Austro-Hungarian throne had not been murdered in Sarajevo. Thinking there would not have been a different excuse for the war's eruption soon after is naïve. After all, the team could have chosen any other path of action. Hence, removing the incentive system would be completely symptomatic. So the only good recommendation in this situation is not creating any change for a while (a principle well rooted in Systemic thinking, as you will see later).

Now, let's see what using Simplicity can offer us in such a complex case.

We are going to use our new arsenal beginning with the Core Analysis technique to locate the core and get an understanding of what is really going on. Locating the core is a bit tricky because some causes may disguise themselves as the core, when in fact they are a response to the core. Differentiating stones from ripples is very simple, but is one of the most common mistakes managers and consultants make in managing change.

It helps to keep the steps of locating cores in mind:

1. Identify causes and secondary results.
2. Set secondary results as the outer circle.
3. Target secondary results and ask why.
4. Establish the answer of the results investigation as a one circle down.
5. Look at causes and ask why (again and again until you can't take it anymore) in response to the circle you've just established.
6. Start from the core and make sure you've covered all the secondary results.
7. If you haven't covered all secondary results go back to step one and look for another core.
8. You're there, but wait… Test it.

It is clear that tension, power struggles, and deceptive behaviors are all caused by something, and so are the responses. Managerial turnover, increase in team size, and a change in the incentive method, on the other hand, can all be causes. At this point it is unclear which cause leads to which response.

Running quickly to step two, you will notice that for now, each secondary result has its own "pond" with its own core. This is because, initially, we cannot be sure that these are the result of one cause.

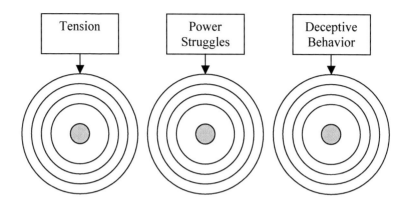

Starting with the obvious results in step three, here are the questions and their possible answers:

- Why are there high levels of tension in the team?—Because of team dynamics/as a result of power struggles/distrust in management/unrealistic expectations/other...
- Why are there power struggles among employees?—Team dynamics/lack of leadership/lack of clarity in structure, expectations/other...
- Why is the relationship with management characterized by deception?—Lack of leadership/ lack of trust in management/ loss of intrinsic motivation/ loss of organizational commitment/other...

From this quick sketch alone you can start building a theory. As in this case, you will often find that secondary results are starting to crystallize around common causes at this stage. Let's assume that our new theory is that there is something in the group's dynamics, and something about the distrust in management that are the causes of this predicament. Quickly review all secondary results. Do you think it is possible that these two causes can be responsible for them? If not, add whatever you feel is missing.

This is where most consulting efforts stop. They look into the dynamics and they find that one of the team members is using domineering behavior to achieve power, and there is a lack of trust in the team. Stopping here is almost always a recipe for failure. Remember, without removing core cause, solutions will be short lived, and other secondary results are bound to come up in unexpected places. I'm repeating this because applying solutions without addressing the core is one of the most common mistakes consultants and managers make. Many managers and consultants stop questioning the process at this stage and draw an action plan. Without finding the core this action plan, designed to respond to the ripples, will lead to frustration.

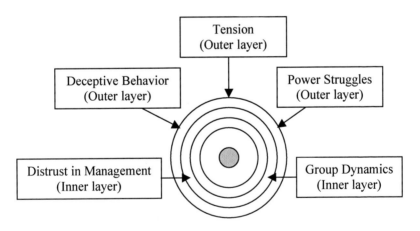

Responding to the ripples without identifying the core, in respect to our case study, can take any of the following shapes:

- Trying to restore trust through workshops, which are designed to be fun without addressing the core.*
- Training the new manager in conflict resolution techniques.
- Applying further changes to restore incentive plans.
- Attempting to restore trust of the senior professional team member by giving him a new formal title and a raise.

It is worse than you think. Not only will these solutions diminish the chances of success, they will now require more money and extend the problems as precious time goes by. We need to take the weed out of the root. We are on a search for a stone, a core, the one cause of all the issues, and the key to success.

Is the loss of trust a core? Can we make do with the difficult task of rebuilding trust in this department? Can you ask why trust is lost or why there are controlling dynamics in the team? Isn't it the role of management to resolve unhealthy dynamics in a team?

We're not there yet, you see. We've made a lot of progress, but these are not core causes!

Now that the picture is starting to appear a bit more clearly, let's look into the causes we couldn't easily characterize as secondary results. Now when we ask why, it would help us to direct the questions at the new information we possess.

---

* It's not that you can't have fun workshops that address the core, it's just that most fun workshops don't.

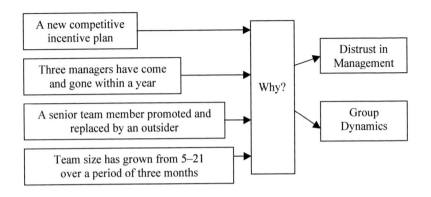

- Why was the new incentive plan a component in losing trust in respect to management?
- Why did the replacement of three managers contribute to lack of trust?
- Why was the promotion and replacement of a senior professional team member a source for losing trust?
- Why was the increase in team size a cause for losing trust?
- Why were these causes contributing to unhealthy group dynamics?

The first thing you can see is instability. There are simply too many changes and that means uncertainty. But ask yourself why is instability and uncertainty related to trust and team dynamics?

This is the kind of question that often feels obvious. Managers just look at me with this, "What do you mean?" look. Now you need to practice Core Analysis and answer questions that seem obvious to you. They are so obvious, in fact, that these managers often can't answer them. This is a good sign. It means we've hit a basic assumption.

For the manager in this case, the answer was direction and communication (in order to assimilate all the input into a theory the manager used Systemic Thinking techniques that we'll go over in part four). It is the absence of direction and communication that allowed a certain team member to manipulate the team's dynamics out of balance and caused a fundamental lack of trust in management. Without communication and direction, the team developed on its own uncertainty, which in turn led to speculation. And instability was proof that things were not about to change because there wasn't anyone in management leading the team in a specific direction.

Okay, so now we have a theory. It's a good theory, but that's all it is.

We can only be confident that we have a true gem when we've tested it. All you need to do is run your theory by your colleagues, employees, and supervisors and get their feedback. Better yet, take your team members on the journey of discovery and you can be sure you're on track. If you are off they will tell you and you will get your final core clear and ready. Now you can base the most effective path of action on this new core.

We've identified the core, but that doesn't make for an effective change. Without an understanding of what needs to be done to change things, it is absolutely insignificant.

I chose this case to practice Simplicity because its absence is so clear. Any one of the changes this department went through coupled with distrust and unhealthy team dynamics, would be a cause for demoralization. The accumulated effect was destructive. When I came in to the picture, it was no longer a matter of rebuilding trust, it was time to deal with a mini disaster. Lack of communication and direction caused a total collapse of the team.

How can a manager approach such a human asset crisis now that things have gone far beyond the core problems? Shouldn't he address the secondary results as well?

I vote for no. Unless you have the time to devote your entire energy to resolving such a crisis (since obviously there are no deadlines for the product or anything...) you're either going to choose where to focus or lack of time will choose for you. It's up to you.

What about the other two Simplicity techniques?

Seeing things as they truly are and Receptiveness are going to help us resolve the challenge. Can you see how lack of trust, deception, lack of direction, and miscommunication thrive when truth is not in evidence? It's time to go back to seeing things as they really are. Once the whole team and its manager live by an interwoven combination of truth and respect, which are established by communication and setting direction, this challenge will be resolved from its core.

In this case, the manager I worked with started by opening a new channel of communication with his staff. All information was to be given to all team members and each private conversation was followed by an email report to the whole team. This meant transparency or eliminating uncertainty (see Beware of Your Own Limitations). Team members were encouraged to make suggestions, and ask questions. The response was always related to content, never by who was the message carrier—not even if the speaker was the manager (see Separate Packaging from Content). When basic assumptions surfaced (in some cases team members expressed their disbelief in change with, "But, you're not going to do anything about it anyway!"), the manager worked with the team to find the sources of these assumptions.

Now team members were part of the decision-making processes.

No one person, regardless of their informal or formal hierarchical position, was assumed to have a better understanding of reality; however, it was clear the manager had to make the decisions. They were constantly asked to bring their opinions and insights up for discussion. Typically, for a distrust challenge, at first it was all about complaints and threats. Gradually, though, team members started adopting a more optimistic and trusting approach.

Furthermore, team members were asked to start seeing things from the manager's perspective, their team member's perspective, and even management's perspective (see Change the Focus of Things). They were asked to make suggestions and base their conclusions on the whole truth rather than their own truth.

Within three months, thanks to the consistency of their manager, this department has turned into one of the company's most creative departments. And secondary results, such as a domineering team member and lack of trust were explicitly resolved. When I checked in a year later, I had learned that turnover had stopped altogether.

Simplicity—Maximizing Human Assets

Now you know how simple it is to see more, focus your effort only on the core of things, and be receptive. I'm sure you are totally committed to integrating it into each and every thing you do. You can use core analysis to analyze anything that isn't working to your full satisfaction. In time, teach that skill and the other Simplicity techniques to your team.

Let's look at the added values that wait for you when you get there—those that are directly related to our two initial goals. You are going to gain all of these wonderful bonuses, without making any additional effort, except for practicing Simplicity. You are not to focus on how to communicate, prevent conflicts, or solve problems. These are the ripples. They will come about naturally when you focus on the basic principles of Simplicity. I'm only covering them here so you will know what to expect.

Simplicity encourages creativity, problem solving, and trust. It opens closed lines of communication, teaches basic skills of influence and negotiation, increases prioritizing skills, planning skills, effective conflict resolution, an ability to respond calmly during pressure, and much more. Top that with an unshakable desire to excel and…

That's what combining kindness with the right set of skills can do.

Simplicity and Building Up a Desire to Excel

Simplicity does better than just preserve the flame of desire to excel. It actually encourages the desire to be stronger. Simplicity leads to wonderful results by building on an equal value of knowledge, bringing the real self to work, creating an emotional anchor, reducing and quickly resolving conflicts, and creating a deep sense that you are being understood.

An equal value of knowledge—Both Receptiveness and seeing things as they truly are will lead to a clear statement: Knowledge is knowledge. It's the same regardless of who thinks it. By admitting to a lack of ownership of knowledge you are making plenty of room for cooperation with your team. This is no longer the "know-it-all" managerial model. You are a part of a team. The only thing that defines you as a manager is your integration position, your authority and the responsibility and accountably that come with it. It is these reasons that lead to your place as the final decision-making person. Since each idea or suggestion is being evaluated in its own right, and because no one person can make it without the team's watchful eye, each individual's contribution is valued. As different people benefit the team in different ways, practicing Simplicity makes the team realize that all are needed in order for the team to succeed as a whole.

This equality of knowledge gives employees a message of objectivity and respect. What they have to say is as important as what anyone else has to say. Hierarchy is no longer used to manipulate power. Logic and content win over politics. Can you imagine how it feels to be part of such a team? To the individual employee it is an opportunity to contribute to the team by no other standards but by thinking creatively, and being inquisitive.

Bringing the real self to work—In a sense, seeing things as they truly are and Receptiveness bring people back to who they are. It promotes an inquisitive, individualistic, anything but programmed, mindset. This means rewarding people for being who they truly are. Most people only get to be their true self around a few very good friends and, if they are very lucky, their spouse and close family. Very few of your employees associate being "real" with how they are at work.

Simplicity takes all of the irrelevant aspects of working together out of the picture (like how much this person reminds you of how you do things, how confident they sound, how they smell and dress—you name it). Ideas are valued separately. In fact, you may find yourself actually liking the ideas of someone you do not enjoy working with. It also means that if their ideas are rejected it's not because you didn't like them, but because they didn't stand the test of everything else the group knows. Since stigma, personal connections and charisma just left the room, people regain the belief that discussions are actually fair and that they can influence the course of things just like the next person.

Creativity is one of the highest forms of self-fulfillment. In order to encourage self-expression and creativity people need to know that though they may be wrong, their truth is considered equal to that of others. By encouraging people to think for themselves and be themselves, you are giving them one of the greatest gifts any manager can give: bringing their real self to work.

Emotional Anchor—Receptiveness, when practiced by the manager and other team members, provides employees with an emotional anchor. It gives the speaker a sense of emotional safety and projects a feeling of respect that one is understood and valued.

For people to feel comfortable with the independence given to them with Real Knowledge and Simplicity, they need to know that this is accompanied by acceptance and understanding. Couple independence with a feeling of rejection and you are not only nipping independence in the bud, you're actually making sure you won't be trusted again. If you've betrayed their trust once, now they'll hesitate to trust you again.

When you experiment, you want to know that if you make a mistake you won't be confronted by anger, humiliation, any sign of aggression, or blame. If the response has a slight hint of threat, it will either be frustrating or it will take time until you will see independence again. There are pleasant, supportive ways to disagree and adequate follow up is a good preventive strategy.

As I mentioned before, intrinsic motivation is one of the most important keys of a successful creative process. Organizations have come to realize their dependency on human emotional and intellectual assets. Creativity, ingenuity, problem-solving, communication, and service are only a few of these invaluable assets organizations cannot survive without. It is important to understand that a creative process, for instance, will not exist in a work environment that is not constructed to encourage it. Since these assets require the deepest contribution an employee can offer, employees need to feel safe and respected if they are to contribute their inner self.

Reducing and quickly resolving conflicts—If you ask me, the real indication of a healthy relationship is not how you normally interact, but how you handle conflict situations. All three Simplicity techniques improve the chances of avoiding an unnecessary conflict, and handling it with finesse. Once managers and their teams start using Simplicity, people listen instead of focusing on what they want to say and how they are going to justify their own point of view. They quickly and effectively look for the core of disagreements and can overcome them, or at least agree to disagree, until they find common ground (Systemic thinking will help there). Employees will start asking for feedback, offering each other pointers, and enjoy thinking together about where things can go wrong.

Fewer conflicts mean fewer reasons to worry about going to work in the morning. Possessing the confidence, that if a conflict might present itself it will be resolved with fairness and without a big emotional explosion will make people look forward to seeing the people they work with.

Make people feel you really understand them—Receptiveness means people are more likely to come talk to you if there is something on their mind. More venting means, at the very least, that there is less emotional baggage threatening to erupt. Team members who do not feel comfortable expressing themselves will open up thanks to a feeling they are really listened to, voicing ideas that would have otherwise stayed in their lower desk drawer.

You'd be surprised to see how talking can surface concerns that would have not even occurred to your employee before, but are burdening them thus, educing their productivity, commitment, and intrinsic motivation. Not to mention that understanding people's needs increases the chances of gaining their trust.

I'm hoping that by now you can really get a sense of how kindness is the only management style that can achieve such incredible results.

Simplicity and the Skills to Excel

In Genesis 2:20, just before God creates Eve from Adam's rib the verse marks, "… and for Adam, there was not found a counter helper."* I've always liked the term counter helper because it embodies the unique union between one frame of thought and its counter thought. It's the ability to counter another person in the most helpful way of togetherness.

Simplicity trains your staff to provide each other with counter assistance. Team members become one another's supervisors, highlighting each other's weaknesses in the most supportive way possible. They'll do this because of two reasons; they are all familiar with the same thinking models, which give them a common language, and they are used to figuring out how to think things through for themselves and bring up disagreements. They do it with you, and they'll duplicate it to other interactions, most

---

* This is a direct translation from Hebrew. Unfortunately when the Bible gets translated it loses a lot of its meanings and here the beautiful "Ezer Kenegdo" which literally translates into "counter helper" was translated into "helper."

easily with people who are under the same training as they.

Your employees are going to ask you and other team members for improvement ideas, checking themselves before acting. They will actively seek feedback (turning them into good feedback receivers) focusing on how to do better in the future instead of hanging on to whether they were right or wrong.

Once you start questioning your own perception of reality, focusing on what you know and what you assume, you have opened the door to healthy communication, conflict prevention, and resolution skills. With some guidance, you will notice your team members start asking each other for their perception of the truth. Understanding other people, from their point of view, is an invaluable skill for teamwork.

Questioning reality and looking for the logic behind results is also a platform for creativity. True creativity and innovation imply independent thinking. Seeing things as they truly are promotes independent thinking because in it hides the encouragement to defy consensus. If you are asking people to reflect on what they see as real, you are basically asking them to go beyond what they are fed. You are encouraging individual thinking, people reaching their own conclusions serves for two vital causes; creativity and a watch dog. Simplicity encourages disagreement, the ability to highlight differences, and create tension, which can be considered a positive force when it is properly directed. Now that your staff is not taking things at face value, do not be surprised if the same skills are transferred to customer service, marketing, sales, and other areas.

Put that inquisitive mind together with the planning skills that follow right behind (thinking your ideas through will do that to you) and you've got alertness. This means your team will now start looking at facts and information, and ask questions such as, "How is this going to affect us?" and "Is this our best action plan when we know this new information about the market?" These are very common secondary responses to Simplicity. Since bringing disagreement up for discussion is common and encouraged, thoughts of such will no longer stay dormant in the minds of your team. Instead, they will be brought to your attention.

Planning (and decision making) is improved further because you are exposed to the things you would have been blind to before. Planning requires a realistic representation of where you are and where you want to go. Clearly, if you are missing some of the facts about either, you will not be able to estimate the required efforts for getting from point A to point B. Learning how to be each other's "counter help" and gaining skills to question what is before them, is naturally followed by the abilities of benefiting from diversity and handling ambiguity. Practicing Simplicity brings openness to different points of view, different cultures, and to the understanding that two opposites often have much in common.

But Simplicity provides more than just one set of skills to deal with conflicts and contradictions. By noticing more levels in a message beyond just words and practicing active listening (reducing judgmental listening) your staff will have better interpersonal communication skills. When people are engaged in a conflict, they are often busy formulating a response to what is being said. They assume that they have heard what their opponent is saying many times before, rather than paying attention they focus on how they can respond to win the argument. Practicing Simplicity bypasses this hurdle.

Finally, Simplicity promotes the ability to distinguish the significant from the insignificant. Do you have an employee who cannot prioritize? Perhaps you have a team member who can't stop perfecting a job when it's time to move on? Through the constant search for cores, your team members can learn the concept of having certain segments of a job weigh more than others.

This is a vital skill when it comes to making decisions on a project management level, but it is as significant for small-scale processes as well. In terms of time management, an inability to know what is important and what can be ignored is the number one problem and there is really no hope of management potential (be it self management or the management of others), if these skills are not addressed.

Need I say more?

Simplicity: Test Yourself

- *I notice facts that contradict my beliefs.*

- *When there is disagreement I am able to see the logic in the opinions of others.*

- *I am able to see that there is more than one right solution to a challenge.*

- *I actively search for opposition to my ideas and conclusions, asking for assistance in finding the flaws to my plans.*

- *I make sure to tell my team if my statement is a fact or an assumption.*

- *I view "good" questions as more important than "good" answers.*

- *Diversity is something I try to learn from.*

- *I encourage my team members to voice new concepts and ideas and enjoy the creativity regardless of applicability.*

- *When I am not fully myself (emotionally or physically) I ask for relevant help.*

- *My team and I often ask for advice and approach team members who might be better at the specific task.*

- *I often practice looking at challenges from different perspectives in order to choose an action path.*

- *I value the content of a message without letting who and how it was presented influence my judgment of the content's value.*

- *When faced with a challenge I locate the core factors that are at play. I then focus all my energy on them.*

- *I encourage my team members to plan an approach for a problem instead of responding quickly with an answer.*

- *While I listen I am focused on the message that is coming across, letting my thoughts and emotions move aside as I absorb what is being said.*

- *When I listen I encourage the speaker to cover all they know about the content by extending the conversation with related questions.*

Part IV

- Straight to the Point
- The First Skill of Kind Excellence—Real Knowledge
- The Second Skill of Kind Excellence—Simplicity
- **THE THIRD SKILL OF KIND EXCELLENCE —SYSTEMATIC THINKING**
- Conclusion

Systemic Thinking Overview

The greatest enemy of any of our truths may be the rest of our truths.
—William James

Simplicity and Real Knowledge will give you the truth, nothing but the truth, but the whole truth, without Systemic Thinking will be out of reach.

Systemic Thinking involves the thinking techniques experts use to build entire mental systems. It's what goes on in the black box of the mind when facts are applied to new insights, solutions, or decisions. It is the integration act that leads to understanding the pieces of the whole in one snapshot.

For reasons that will soon be clear, Systemic Thinking uses subconscious rather than conscious thinking; it uses tension, integrating aspects of time and space.

Unfortunately, it's a type of thinking* none of us learned in school. So when novices come across complex, nonlinear challenges in which they are required to integrate numerous details, they often resort to guessing. But this thinking skill can and should be taught. And that's what we'll spend our time doing in this part of the book.

Systemic Thinking is first and foremost a way of thinking. It is an elusive way of thinking, and hence many professionals confuse it with decision-making processes or creative thinking techniques. Systemic Thinking is neither. We'll start by defining what it really is.

---

* That's right, despite what your fourth-grade teacher might have told you about thinking and day dreaming, subconscious processing is as much a thinking process as conscious thinking is.

Systemic Thinking is made of two techniques that work together:

- Working with tension.
- Awakening the subconscious.

These two techniques are the heart of Systemic Thinking. Thanks to the mastery of these two techniques experienced managers draw decisions, inventors come up with new ideas, and employees learn how to improve. It's only when we use these two techniques that we are able to understand whole nonlinear systems.

Notice that I keep saying "understanding" systems rather than "seeing" whole system. As you'll soon see, Systemic Thinking is not about breaking down the system into as many pieces as possible and finding the interactions between them. By going about it this way, you will actually be further from understanding nonlinear systems as a whole. Instead, we will use the two Systemic Thinking techniques to identify the system's operational codex.

We'll conclude part four by exploring the unique application Systemic Thinking has in human systems. Human systems are different than other nonlinear systems. Therefore, we'll need to understand how Systemic Thinking works to maximize your team's potential in increasing the system's ability to improve itself.

Experts use these techniques instinctively because over the years they had many opportunities to practice. What we want to accomplish here is to shorten your team's learning curve by increasing your understanding and exposure to Systemic Thinking. It takes years to acquire Systemic Thinking if you leave learning to the learner. It takes months at most when you deliberately train yourself and others to use it.

Ready? Let's go.

Chapter Nine

Defining Systemic Thinking

I REMEMBER THE FIRST TIME I heard of Systemic Thinking.* It was a new buzz word and in no time everyone was saying it and doing it; everyone but me. I read books and participated in professional workshops (everything from the theory of constraints through chaos and systems theories to lateral thinking and neuro-linguistic programming) and talked about it to every expert I could find. But though I felt it was very important, I could not figure it out.

Intellectually, I understood the definitions of Systemic Thinking as it was portrayed in the works about the topic. But in retrospect, I know they were just vague descriptions of a skill that unless you already had, you were getting very little insight into practicing. To me they were missing the one part I was looking for, a technique that addresses the thinking change required when moving from "regular" thinking to Systemic Thinking.

So gradually, with lots of practice and a bag full of questions

---

* Systemic Thinking isn't Systems Thinking. These are two different approaches. Both aim to achieve the same thing, but each is based on different basic assumptions, which result in learning different skills. I much prefer Systemic Thinking when it comes to complex nonlinear systems, which is basically true for any human asset management challenge, or any decision or innovation that taps in on the hidden resources of our brain. For more information about the differences between the two, visit www. kindexcellence.com

I set out on a new journey. It's a journey that started with theory and ended with revolutionary Real Knowledge skills. I'm about to travel with you through the minds of those who use Systemic Thinking and show you the elusive thinking skills themselves, the exercise your mind needs in order to create systems. This way you will be able to use these understandings at will.

We'll take a closer look at the definition of Systemic Thinking. We'll track down the thinking process itself and define what this thinking process is aiming for in its most natural state. The idea is that if we'll get your staff to know how Systemic Thinking works, and what it's out to achieve, there will be nothing standing in their way from practicing it whenever needed.

A Type of Thinking, Not a Thinking Structure

Out of clutter, find simplicity. From discord, find harmony. In the middle of difficulty, lies opportunity.

—Albert Einstein

Let's look at the structure of a decision making process.

This is a five-step process that leads you step by step from your goal to the best way to achieving it. You are going to try and look at as many aspects of the system as possible and mapping as much of the interactions you can find. But it isn't Systemic Thinking.

This is where it gets confusing. A decision-making process is ineffective without Systemic Thinking, but that doesn't mean they are one and the same. The truth is, you can use Systemic Thinking or choose to ignore it when you go through a decision making process. You can go through the whole process and use only logic and analysis, never integrating once. One option will lead to superb results, while the other will be mediocre at best.

If you look closely you'll notice that in each one of the steps outlined for decision-making, you need to use a form of integrative thinking. You need it when you decide which data is relevant and which you are going to ignore. You use it again when you need to extract meaning from what is before you. And you keep using it all the way to choosing and applying your chosen option.

Systemic Thinking is the mental ability to quickly integrate complex, nonlinear systems into a single understanding. It's the thinking process we use when we estimate if it would be safe to bypass another car on the road, and when we decide to choose a certain organizational vision over another. It is a movement from a multilevel scattered form of data representation to a single narrow perspective of choice.

Simply put, it's our mental ability to integrate everything we know into a single insight.

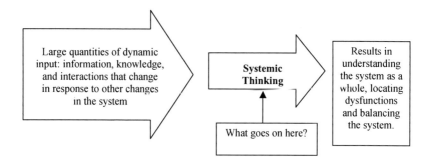

Most professionals do not acknowledge this type of thinking, nor do they know how to activate it. Because of how we were taught to think, what they are really doing is going through the whole process using two contradicting thinking processes at once. One skill set, analytical, logical, and focused, is trying to overcome the natural synthesizing, integrating other. But you should know that there are times and cases when analysis is the best tool for the job, while there are other times that call for a different type of thinking. We need to learn how to activate this other type of thinking, recognize where and when it's needed, and start cashing in on it. This other type of thinking isn't new. It's being used to train Taoist monks, military commanders, composers, artists and others. You can dismiss it and think that it doesn't belong in the business world, but you would be wrong. Systemic Thinking is the skill behind any integration thinking. You can fight it or make the most of it. It's up to you.

Why is this important to train business people to use Systemic Thinking?

As I said before, successful executives learn to use Systemic Thinking over time. They hardly ever recognize using it, but they do nonetheless. Actively training managers to use Systemic Thinking shortens the learning curve dramatically. This improves their ability to make effective decisions, understand and improve their human assets and work processes, innovate and strategize much sooner than they would have otherwise.

Although shortening managers' learning curves and speeding up employee training is of great significance already, that's hardly all of it. Learning how to use Systemic Thinking means we can train novices, and managers that are not capable of producing these skills for themselves. Not everyone is talented at developing skills, but often not being able to develop a skill is not an indicator of the ability to learn it and practice it. These are very different abilities. So now we can give managers and employees that cannot develop Systemic Thinking themselves accessibility to this wonderful skill.

Furthermore, Real Knowledge can be tested and improved. That means we can look at the individual skills our experts have spontaneously developed and improve them. We can take these excellent individuals and get them to be even better.* We can do it because, once on the surface, skills can be upgraded and tested more objectively then presented back to experts. These already productive individuals become even more effective because now they have an upgraded version of their own technique.

As you'll see in chapter ten, Systemic Thinking requires an understanding of a whole new way of thinking. Its best when applied through subconscious rather than conscious thinking, it flourishes in the presence of tension, and it must take time and space into account. Systemic Thinking works very differently from any other form of thinking. It has its own rules. At its core, Systemic Thinking is all about integration.

How Does Systemic Thinking Work?

If it were up to analytical thinking to handle complex nonlinear systems its first inclination would be to break things down. Systemic Thinking gathers information in a very different way. As you'll soon discover, gathering information is more like collating than collecting.

Collating the System's Activation Codex

Systemic Thinking is not about trying to specify all the details and gluing them together. Instead it has a different goal; it funnels

---

* It's much more difficult to get from 91% to 95% productivity than to get from 60% to 80% productivity. And when you do the increase in benefit is monumental in effect. A real genius in improvements of this kind is Gary Bartlett of Productivity Solutions International. For more about his work go to www.prodsol.co.nz

large bodies of information to locate only the determining factors of a given system.

If detectives were to investigate a crime scene using analytical thinking they would systematically go through all the details they could find. A detective using Systemic Thinking would go straight to the most significant factors. A manager using analytical thinking to resolve a challenge would ask to know everything about the problem, but a manager using Systemic Thinking would instantly know to focus only on the factors that will help resolve it.

It may surprise you to know that when experts use Systemic Thinking they do not actually base their decisions on all of the information they can collect. In fact, they do not even base their decisions on most of the input before them. Instead, in order to understand a whole system, their mind quickly funnels through the whole stack vigorously searching for the few factors that best define the system.*

You actually use this aspect of Systemic Thinking more often than you would think. You do because it's the most effective way of thinking for certain challenges, and because no one discouraged you from using it in those life regions.

Do you know the feeling that you are certain who the criminal is after watching only fifteen minutes of your favorite detective series? How do we do that?

Chances are you have picked up on the clues that the producer keeps sending you each week. You do not know what in the way things are presented leads you to that conclusion, but your mind has seen certain patterns enough times to produce that response. What you are noticing is that every time the producer tries to make it seem like one of the characters is insignificant to the plot;

---

*   There are many researches about this topic. A popular collection of these can be found in the book *Blink* by Malcolm Gladwell. Mr. Gladwell refers to the action of funneling through the numerous details as "thin slicing."

it's that character you know you should suspect.

What you're seeing is a pattern that defines the way that specific producer likes to build a story. We all have these codes. Systems, and that includes human systems, have an operational guide. These are a set of preprogrammed orders that subconsciously tell us how to think and act. Organizational consultants call these basic assumptions, and I'll refer to them here, by borrowing a biological term, as the system's DNA.

All we have to do here is highlight the thinking process you're already using and duplicate it to the business situations that so desperately need it.

Most functioning systems (with the exception of chaotic systems to the best of our knowledge) include an organized activation codex. That codex, like a person's DNA specifies all of the basic assumptions, the operational orders if you please, that the system obeys to. These elusive pieces of information lead us to specific understandings, conclusions, choices, decisions, and actions. They are like the system's DNA, telling the system when, how, and why.

These are the significant factors experts subconsciously look for when they master Systemic Thinking. Find the operational mechanism and you'll find the system.*

This activation codex, however, is hidden from view. It is locked behind doors of awareness, shaded by a feeling that it's too obvious to even question. You do not know why you suspect a certain character as the criminal, you are not aware of noticing the pattern there, and yet you draw a conclusion. In all likelihood

---

* As I already mentioned earlier, systems often have operational orders that contradict and compete with other orders in the same system. Understanding how and why these operate is one of the keys to creating balanced systems.

the producer himself isn't aware of his own thinking patterns.

It may have been very difficult to locate this activation codex, only you have one powerful thing working for you. Like DNA, the hidden logic of the system is found in each and every one of its sub units. Not all the codex is active in each unit, but at least one segment is, and there are a limited number of codes, which can be found relatively quickly.

You can find the activation codex by comparing different units within the same system, looking into the repetitions and contradictions. By crosschecking behaviors and facts you'll find the common theme or the hidden explanation that stems from these two structures. And the system's DNA segment is revealed.

Where to Find the System's DNA?

The meaning of words lays in the connections between letters.

—Kabala

An activation codex is well hidden in between the elements and interactions of a system. But it's actually much easier to find it than many managers imagine.

The main challenge managers have to face is relearning how to look at systems. Once they're able to let go of old habits, locating these hidden system segments becomes very simple. Managers are used to analyzing systems. They break the system down to its most refined elements, they chart interactions, and in connecting them they hope to see the system. Unfortunately, this effort makes it more difficult to understand the system as a whole. Breaking things down, categorizing them and putting them in a structure, takes you further away from making connections because your mind is too busy in analysis to engage in synthesis. The codex is in between the elements and interactions, and no amount of defining the elements and interactions themselves is going to get you closer to it.

The easiest and fastest way to identify a system's hidden activation codex is by looking at contradictions and repetitions in the system. We can't extract the actual meaning of the codex segment just yet, for that we'll need the help of tension and of our subconscious, but we can identify its location.

As I mentioned, the codex is hidden in between units, and the ones easiest to crosscheck are repetitions and contradictions.

Repetitions

Suppose you saw someone sketching on a piece of paper. The drawing, you notice, includes the finest details. Then you meet that person for lunch and you notice they rearrange their napkin and their utensils so that these are aligned with the edges of the table. In comparing these two situations you have learned something about this person.

That something is a segment of their system's codex. You may not be sure how to attach meaning and interpret what you just saw, and we'll go over that soon. But if this person has an operational codex that leads them to being accurate, manifestations of this codex are likely to appear in many of this person's behaviors.

We do not always see the whole codex in each connection we make, but we always see a segment of it. Run these connections enough times, collect enough observations and you've got the system right there.

By identifying repetitions your staff can quickly come to understand systems. This means that if they find a nonlinear complex system to function at less than its optimal potential (and that includes a project they are involved in, a dissatisfied customer, or the person in the mirror) they can now start to see what is stopping the system from excellent results.

Contradictions

You are interviewing candidates for a secretarial position. You want them to be reliable, have a high customer service orientation, be efficient, be able to self manage and be a team player. How do you go about finding out if the candidate before you possesses these gems?

Conventional interviewing techniques have questions designed for each personality aspect; Systemic Thinking looks for DNA segments.

The most effective way to figure it out is to locate contradictions in the way a person presents himself and ask him to explain how things fit together. Let's say this person has worked in a single job for six years and after that he kept skipping from one job to the next every year or so. A different person started her career working for high tech companies and then switched to working only for nonprofits. For another candidate you feel there is a big gap between how he presents himself on paper and how he comes across in person. Or perhaps you see that while everything else in a candidate's resume is described in short one sentence structure, a single bullet is emphasized and elaborated.*

These are all contradictions you can set up to draw meaning from.

And you can also go on and combine contradictions with repetitions.

When you talk to the fourth candidate, the one with the

---

* You can find more about the applications of Kind Excellence skills to interviewing and other managerial challenges under the Kind Excellence skills course at www.kindexcellence.com.

elaborated bullet, does he exhibit the same differences in behavior when he talks about the different topics in person? Does the person who skipped from job to job keep jumping from one topic to the next? And does he seem scattered? Does the candidate that switched from high tech to nonprofits have other values that somehow echo that behavior?

These will reveal at least one segment of the candidate's individual operational codex.

If the candidate left the high tech industry because she wanted to have time for her hobbies or family, that's a DNA segment. If the reason she left the high tech industry for nonprofits was a lack of focus around goals, then that too would affect the way she operates. Each one of these will affect how these candidates perform as a secretary because basic assumptions guide us across situations, not just per a specific case.

Whether it's from contradictions or repetitions, the way to extract the meaning of a DNA segment is the same. You take a couple of elements and you figure out why and how they co-exist. Later you will couple another pair elsewhere in the system and get a new understanding. Bit by bit you will have the whole operational codex before you.

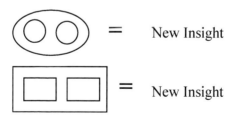

When we'll talk about extracting meaning in chapter ten you'll see that the idea is that you take two unrelated well-defined elements and you try to explain why they both exist in the system. You do not want to know how they interact, what we're saying here is that the two exist in the same system and we want to know why the system "chooses" to keep both there.

Looking for the operational codex of human systems is not restricted to the individual level. You can apply the same technique to understand the operational codex of teams and organizations.* It is also important to understand that applying Systemic Thinking isn't for the manager to play solo. Like any other technique in this book Systemic Thinking is designed to be a skill you both practice and train your staff to use as often as possible.

Where and How Can You and Your Team Get Practice?

As you recall Systemic Thinking is a Real Knowledge skill. It is a technique that once acquired can be applied to many challenges. As such, it is always best practiced in small doses of everyday challenges. There are many practice opportunities on every level, you just need to keep your eyes open and they'll literally fall in your lap.

Take this team level example, for instance.

Let's pretend you just started a new position as the head of a development department at a new organization. Obviously you were very successful at your previous job.

The first things you see when you start are the differences. Your old department used to do things this way and this department does it that way. Being a manager for quite some time now, you've heard that it's a good idea to wait a while before making any

---

* You can also apply these principles to other nonlinear complex systems other than human systems. It is after all a Real Knowledge skill!

changes, and that because of the differences in organizational culture and of functional differences in the system you should be cautious in changing things before you fully understand how the system works.

So the challenge is to understand how your new department works. How do people interact, what are the processes related to information and knowledge, teamwork and other aspects. You could start analyzing the system, getting to know each individual team member, the interactions in the different teams, the structure of information flow, or you could save a lot of time and do it right. You can skip most of this and get a better understanding of the system by locating your new department's operational codex.

Say the department is made of three development teams. You notice that in team one people constantly feel they need to come to you directly with questions, while in team two it's the team leader who'll present the team's questions to you. These are two defined elements, and you can see a contradiction here. One works one way and the other works differently. Now you discover another contradiction, the two departments differ in the level of professional knowledge required from team members. You have a few contradictions, and some repetition. Ask yourself: Why do they appear? Why does the difference in professionalism manifest itself in using these different communication channels? The next chapter will give you excellent techniques to start working on these questions, and once you'll reveal the answers you'll be holding a segment of this team's operational codex.

If you find that your predecessor saw no point in addressing the team leader in team one because the team leader there isn't familiar with the details to the extent his individual team members are, you found something of value. This is a defining activation assumption that guides the way this system (i.e. this department) operates.

This DNA segment is likely to apply to other areas of difference between the two teams. For instance, it is possible that team two responds better to clear instructions, and team one doesn't. It's possible that since team members in team one feel they are more knowledgeable about the details of their project than their team leader, they will not like changing things or applying new ideas if they are not consulted. Do you see how one basic assumption can affect many system behaviors?

These are of course only assumptions, and you will need to see them more than once to establish a pattern (or at least test them with people in the team) but that's a great opportunity to practice right there.

There are more dramatic and less dramatic examples all around you. Next time one of your employees asks you how to deal with a dissatisfied client, talk to him about Systemic Thinking. If you notice your secretary is having a difficult time prioritizing, show her what it takes to know what is more important at any given moment. Plug in Systemic Thinking skills whenever you can.

Anyone in the team can apply Systemic Thinking techniques to any human system, at any level, and all the time.

Look at any process or challenge that human beings take part in. Look at staff meetings, time management, prioritizing patterns, programming sequence etc. Anything your team does even how your secretary answers the phone is good practice material when you're looking for DNA segments.

What Can Kind Excellence Skills Do for You?
A Success Story

I was part of team of consultants who was asked to help the sales department of one of the industry's biggest pharmaceutical companies through the tides of a merger.

The unit I was working with belonged to the company that had been bought. And since the approach of the company that took over was to apply its values over the ones of the purchased company, this department's management, sales agents, and staff felt confused and frustrated.

By working with this team to compare their values and the values of the purchasing company the team was able to understand the destructive response it had. Exposing the team to its own operational codex liberated its members from a vicious cycle. The team ended up with an even more productive set of values that stemmed from the contradictions of these two value sets. I was able to diminish the frustration, give the team its sense of control back, and stay totally committed to the new value set.

I only regret how new Kind Excellence concepts were to me at the time. I should have thought of the benefits the purchasing management team would have gotten from understanding Kind Excellence skills. If they could only come to understand that their approach was missing an unusual opportunity to learn from the differences (after all, the company they bought was successful enough to compete against them for years). Live and learn.

Let's look at your team's workflow for a moment. What are the contradictions that present themselves? What is common? What can explain the coexistence of these contradictions? Do not look at the design of the workflow because we do not care about the structure of who does what before whom here. We just want to know why two contradicting elements simultaneously exist, and what is the one reason that allows two elements or contrasting forces to work together?

This is a significant difference. While mapping the different elements and their interactions will give us a sense of how things work, looking for patterns will tell us a lot about why they interact the way they do. Once we see which DNA segments activate your system we'll know if you take slack time into account, whether or not workload is distributed appropriately (such as realizing that a team member is constantly taking on more than they can accomplish, or that another team member can do more). That's a great deal of improvement Systemic Thinking can offer us just by focusing on workflow alone.

Got it?

Super.

So far we saw how to identify contradictions and repetitions. That's the first step to Systemic Thinking. By uncovering these structures our mind is faced with at least two factors that are far enough apart to produce a new insight. This new insight is either an understanding of a pattern that units the repetitive behaviors or an explanation for the co existence of the contradicting factors.

Once presented with these structures our mind has an opportunity to overcome the gap by working with the tension that has been created, and look for the answer to this enigma by drawing on everything it knows so far. This leads us directly to the two techniques of Systemic Thinking: working with tension and awakening the subconscious.

Chapter Ten

Systemic Thinking Techniques

THOSE OF US WHO were lucky went through school learning something about analytical thinking. Very few indeed learned anything about applying integration to their thinking process. But integrating is vital. Unfortunately for most, and most fortunately for the few who know how to apply it, integration and synthesis use completely different thinking processes and techniques and obey completely different rules. If you know how to work with integration, you are very lucky indeed.

Very few managers notice contradictions and repetitions, and even fewer know how to use them to extract meaning. Is there a structure, a process to extract meaning or is it all experience? Once you notice a repetitive behavior such as painting in detail and rearranging the napkin, can you use a method to extract the meaning of this behavior or do you have to be an expert to know what pattern (i.e. perfectionism, obsessive behavior, high attention to details, all three or perhaps something all together different) should be associated with this repetition?

Extracting meaning certainly improves with learned experience, providing that learning is coupled with accurate feedback*. But

---

* Without an effective feedback system, you cannot know if your interpretation was correct, in which case experience can build false conclusions.

since experience can be separated from Systemic Thinking one can practice Systemic Thinking with or without it. You can always come up with a few theories and then test them or run them by an expert. The more you do this the faster you'll learn. The more your staff does this, the faster they will learn.

In order to extract meaning from contradictions or identify patterns by looking at repetitions, experts use two leading techniques: they work with tension, and they use their subconscious.

So far we've presented our mind with different elements instructing it to draw commonalities. But we can do better than give our mind a direct order. We can put it in the right receptive mode, and facilitate the thinking for it. In this chapter I'm going to show you how to extract meaning and see connections.

It's as simple as ABC.

Working with Tension

Tension is a great thing.

Don't laugh, I really mean that!

Tension is the "substance" that resides in between elements. It's tension that draws electrons to protons, and its tension that repels two electrons when they are together. It's tension that gives motion a motivation to exist. It emphasizes where we are and where we can be, and exposes us to our blind spots. It's only thanks to contradictions and the distance between elements that we can enjoy any form of art, or feel anything to begin with. It's tension that is directly related to any form of creativity.

I must admit that transforming tension into a system is one of my personal favorites. The understanding of using tension as a building force is a wonderful magical process. Using tension is lots of fun if you enjoy riddles. With the right approach and skills, resolving tension often feels like Eureka, a moment of emotional uplift.

The first technique for extracting meaning from contradictions and repetitions is the understanding of how to work with tension. It is a deep understanding of how to locate the activation codex of the system, to find those few DNA segments that instruct the system into action. You've already created tension when you looked into contradictions and repetitions, now you just need to use it to build meaning.

Tension is great if you know how to use it to your benefit, and I intend to show you how.

Maximizing the Potential of Tension

I do not paint things. I paint the difference between things.
—Henri Matisse

The first thing you want to do when you are working with tension is to stretch it out. I say this because most managers, in their desire to resolve a challenge will do anything but prolong tension. Most managers' first reaction is, in fact, counter productive. They eliminate tension as soon as they possibly can.

This elimination takes many forms. Some managers try to resolve tension by ignoring it. Others do not even allow it to arise. Another common form of tension slaughter is the strong desire to move straight into action, find the solution and fix things before there was any time to understand the challenge at hand.

But before we talk about how to maximize tension, let's look at its number one killing widespread convention: that two contradicting facts can't both be right.

It's a shame managers believe this because according to Systemic Thinking principles, allowing two contradiction to be true builds tension, and tension is the most significant factor for growth, improvement, innovation, and progress.

And it's unfortunate, because it's dead wrong.

Let me explain what I mean.

Place a rose in the center of a circle of mirrors. Each mirror will hold a different image of the rose. Each mirror is describing the truth, and to it it's the whole truth. To a mirror it would be inconceivable that any other mirror sees anything else.*

Just because what you see is correct, does not mean someone else is not seeing correctly too. In order for a group of people to see the whole picture, or the system if you please, team members need to investigate the tension, the differences, the commonalities and the definitions of their reality under the assumption that all of the information has a valid reason to exist.

You might end up realizing, as you discuss things, that one of the members is influenced by wrong assumptions. It's like what would happen if one of the mirrors argued that there is a smudge on the rose, when in fact the smudge is on the mirror itself. The smudge, though dislocated, is part of reality too.

If you decide that you are holding what's real in your palm, then you have already chosen one end- yours. This means there is no room for another side to exist. Hence, there is no tension, no potential, no growth, and except for shortening the process no benefit at all.

It's critical, then, to let tension work its way through a challenge. Using tension effectively goes even further beyond letting tension take its course, it dictates expanding tension.

This is really important because tension is a unique material, with special defining qualities. In ignorant hands it is a source of stress and confusion but in skilled hands it's more precious for growth than anything else.

---

* Thank you, Diana Kipping, for this beautiful analogy on perception.

How Can You Increase Tension?

In order to solve this differential equation you look at it until a solution occurs to you.

—George Polyá

There are two basic tactics to intensify tension: compare what you know with what you are still missing, which I call knowledge vs. void bouncing, and getting your mind to work and rest interchangeably.

Knowledge vs. void bouncing— In order to understand how this technique works, let's borrow from math for a moment.

Look at the following equations:

$$Y = 6$$
$$Z = 17$$
$$X + Y = Z$$
$$X = ?$$

We all know this one, you plug Y and Z in and—wait, freeze for a moment. Suppose this wasn't simple math, and that you could not subtract 6 from 17, you just had to stare at $X + 6 = 17$ and reach the answer… no subtraction I said… what is your brain doing now?

It's running around going 6, 17, 6, 17… void… 6, 17, 6, 17… void. If you do that long enough 11 will appear. Note that some people think 9 is the missing component. That's fine. You do not have to always see the missing information yourself, and you can run it by people and compare it to other insights. The important thing is to practice the technique. Time and practice coupled with testing your results will give you an 11 every time.

When you ask your brain; "What makes fact A and fact B

work together?" Your brain is producing a link that wasn't there before; "They do because..." and that's a new understanding that is one step closer to being useful.

Let's suppose you are interviewing someone for a job again. You realize this person is a perfectionist and that they do not take criticism very well. Let these be Y. Now you know what the job is like, what it requires, the people this person will need to work with. Assign Z to those. All you need to do is place them next to each other:

$$Z - Y = X$$

Does the equation work?

You can apply this technique to contradictions and repetitions as well. When you present your brain with such equations, tension will do the rest.

If you do not see the answer, just run your brain between the two inputs. As you'll soon see this type of thinking gets your subconscious engaged, and no one can extract meaning like the subconscious.

Contract and release—This technique is designed to bounce your brain and get it to function in a higher capacity. Here the tension is magnified by the states of focus and lack of focus.

As long as the other thing you're doing is totally unrelated you're creating the desired tension. Focus needs to be followed by some type of mental rest (and for all of you out there seeing this as an excuse to watch TV all day, remember that mental rest is great but it has to be followed by another session of focus).

You may want to schedule a five-minute "thinking session" right before you go out to lunch, or before you go out to a party.

But you can also use other non-curricular activities like painting or singing for a few minutes before you focus again.

The main idea here is to rest and focus interchangeably.*

Now I'm sure you wonder what comes next. If you've stayed with me this far I'm sure there is very little I can do to surprise you, but let's try this anyway:

You do nothing. Once you have tension buzzing and bubbling, just let go.

Our mind works whether we direct it or not. When our mind is confronted with a challenge it spontaneously starts engaging with the challenge moving the different aspects of the challenge around in a desire to make sense. Contradiction, paradox, and defined elements that are far enough apart can create tension. And tension, if left to sauté, "wants" to be resolved.

In physics any two interacting elements that are pulled apart have a "desire" to pull back together, it is called positive potential. Think about two magnets of opposite poles pulled away from each other (and yet kept close enough so that they can still affect each other and be part of the same system). Think of a brick pulled away from the ground—the brick's height becomes part of its potential equation, it becomes energy that "wants" to pull back and return to the ground.

The same applies to different elements in the same human asset system. People are part of a system that has conflicting opinions will feel best if the tension is somehow resolved. Teams that work together on different parts of a development or manufacturing process wish things could go smoothly. The frustration employees and mangers feel when things are not resolved is the best evidence for the need to resolve tension. They may not have the skills to successfully resolve the tension (we'll

---

* People vary in the length of intervals that work best for them.

deal with that in the following two chapters), but the desire to resolve it is alive nevertheless.

It is a good thing to know about tension, and we'll meet it again when we talk about balancing human systems, that tension doesn't like to be over encouraged. It's better at times to let our mind work for us without having us breathe down its neck like an overly controlling mother.

Staying in tension and doing nothing is counterintuitive for many managers. They are programmed to respond fast, resolve, propel, change, and get results. They do not have patience (and according to the majority no "objective" time either) to linger. I encourage you to go back to the Save Time to Make Time principle to relearn how wasteful it is to go fast in these cases.

Once you presented yourself with contradictions and repetitions, at the very moment you directed your mind to locate the hidden operational codex enigma, another force has joined your quest. You have presented it with an invitation and it obliged. Your subconscious has been with you all along.

Acknowledging the Subconscious

Those things that nature denied to human sight, she revealed to the eyes of the soul.

—Ovid

The abilities of the subconscious are very different from those of our conscious mind. Our conscious thinking, which works while our brain is producing beta waves, is our focused, narrow thinking. In this wavelength we are concentrated, linear, and detail oriented. It is an effective thinking mode for focusing on one thing at a time.

"I call it the 'one way mind', because in this state we tend to be certain there is only one way to think about something, and we like to get right to the point... it does not deal well with change. The conscious mind loves stability and will do whatever necessary on the surface to achieve it," writes Dawna Markova, Ph.D. in *The Open Mind.*

This type of thinking is obviously not the best fit for Systemic Thinking.

The subconscious is different. When our brain produces alpha waves we use our subconscious thinking to explore options, experiment, and be receptive.

"It is thinking in dualities, a two-way mode... in fact this way of thinking is vital for decision-making and image making," writes Markova.

This type of thinking is often experienced as mind wandering, or spacing out. We often dismiss subconscious thinking. If it's not focused and goal oriented, we think it's not productive. But it just so happens that this type of thinking is vital in order to establish direction, build a vision, and draw decisions.

If we are expected to understand complex, non-linear, and dynamic systems, we need the subconscious on board.

But how do you get the subconscious to play along?

When tension calls, the subconscious answers. You do not need to do anything about it; it's effortless. All you need is to acknowledge it, and let it be without allowing the conscious to regroup.

The part our subconscious loves more than anything else in systems is contradictions and puzzles. Present yourself with an enigma that your logic and conscious mind can't decipher, and your subconscious will instantly take over. When you highlighted the contradictions and repetitions in the system, you've already extended a very powerful invitation. And unless you dismissed the subconscious, it has been with you since.

Notice what happens to your brain when you confront it with

an impossible or confusing situation. It goes back and forth, jumps between the different components of the contradiction (or the different elements presented to it), and tries to make sense of it. Your subconscious automatically goes into a mode of searching for the system's activation codex. It is looking for commonalities, for the most significant factors for dealing with the challenge. It's buzzing around, wondering, and searching, trying to extract meaning.

Give this famous Koan attributed to Hakuin Ekaku a try:

"Two hands clap and there is a sound; what is the sound of one hand?"

If you do not allow your alert conscious state to take over, your brain will practice a certain natural thinking pattern that engages the subconscious. Do you recognize it?

And how about the following sentence by Dagwood (from a *Blondie* comic strip):

"You know it makes a lot of sense if you don't think about it."

Can you feel it running around in there?

That's the kind of thinking that is required when you need to extract meaning from a nonlinear, complex, dynamic system. It's not something the goal-oriented mindset of the conscious mind can achieve.

But the actual process of extracting meaning is, as befitting the subconscious, out of our direct control.

Knowing who the suspect is in your favorite TV show isn't something you can control. When you decided that the pattern of the overly organized guy you had lunch with in the previous chapter is obsessive, you can't put your finger on how you reached this conclusion. You can't because the subconscious gave you that answer by integrating too many factors for your conscious mind to understand.

That's the way our integrating mind works.

In the book *Accelerated Learning for the 21st Century,* Collin Rose and Malcolm J. Nicholl go over an interesting aspect of genius thinking patterns. These geniuses, a group of phenomenal individuals, claim to have reached their greatest concepts while using one or another form of being in a subconscious state. Einstein attributes his inventions to a state of "fantasy," Beethoven said about his ideas: "they come to me in the silence of the night or in the early morning, stirred into being my moods." Others say they get a flash of insight when they are "half asleep" or doing something totally unrelated such as calmly listening to music.

But wait a moment there, if extracting meaning is controlled by the subconscious then it's a spontaneous process, where is the technique here?

Here is the thing, we can't force the subconscious to extract meaning and understand systems, but we can get it to exercise and get in better shape. It's true there is little you can do to make a horse drink, but if you drag him to water and the horse is thirsty, and the water looks so tempting… what do you think is going to happen?

We can't make our subconscious produce new ideas, extract meaning, or integrate numerous inputs into a coherent understanding, but there are techniques we can use to make sure the invitation is powerful enough to get the subconscious engaged.

By practicing the first step to Systemic Thinking, exposing yourself to contradictions and repetitions, you've already activated your subconscious, got it to wake up and tune in. Just keep it rolling and let the subconscious do its thing. It is a simple, easy to learn and practice technique.

That sums up the two Systemic Thinking techniques, but there is one more thing we need to look at before we can see how this magnificent skill applies to maximizing human assets. The type of systems we're talking about here are dynamic. This means things keep changing, constantly influencing each other. I am including this brief overview here because without the understanding of the effect time and space have on applying change, Systemic Thinking would be incomplete.*

Kind Excellence Tip #7
Move on and then look back

This principle is another way to understand the power of subconscious thinking.

I first noticed this principle when I started studying physics. Each time a new concept was introduced I struggled to get by. My brain just could not figure out what everyone was talking about. Then a week or two would pass, and as we started thinking of more complex examples everything suddenly clicked in my brain. I tagged along like this every semester, starting off really confused and scattered, but passing with flying colors by the end.

I noticed the same phenomenon when I worked as a math tutor to pay for tuition. Along with lots of encouragement and faith in my students' ability to succeed, I pushed my students to take on more complicated materials even though they had not mastered the lower-level skills yet. Then, after a couple of sessions we would go back and look at old problems they were struggling with. It was unbelievable how easy it suddenly seemed to them.

I later discovered that the key to this phenomenon is that the subconscious keeps working long after we have moved on. If we keep providing it with clues to resolve what has puzzled us, it will create more connections and eventually lead us to an understanding of whatever it was we were missing.

---

* There are many references for these two principles especially in Chaos theories and under Systems Thinking applications.

Understanding Change Through Time and Space

I wonder if you are familiar with the wonderful butterfly effect associated with the work of Edward Lorenz in the fabulous Chaos theory. The theory describes a butterfly flapping its wings on one side of the world. The flapping creates a dramatic change in the weather system on the other side of the world. It comes to show that small variations of the initial condition of a system in which causes are dynamic and not directly linked to results (which basically describes anything in which people take part in) may produce large scale and even dramatic variations in the long term behavior of the system. Now these are big words, but it comes to show you how things connect, and how little we know of how things connect.

Kind Excellence Tip #8
Space and Systemic Thinking

This idea is well established in Systems Thinking, and Chaos models. The concept is that in complex systems (ones that are not defined by a straight line between cause and effect) an action in one department or one of the projects in a department, can affect other projects or other departments in ways that we may be blind to. Any action can affect things in parts distant from the cause.

We already know we have a tendency to see only a part of reality, and I think, when it comes to human systems, we only see a small fraction. Though it might be useful to draw charts and maps and increase the awareness to this blindness, I highly recommend you have meetings with different clients and providers (inside your organization too of course) and use the meetings for this purpose: inform and investigate how what you are doing affects others.

Simple.

And then there is time.

Misunderstanding the influence of time on systems and changes within systems in particular is one of the leading troublemakers regarding Systemic Thinking. In these cases the manager tries to influence a situation in a certain direction trying to create change. But once change lingers, managers add an extra effort in the same direction leading to an overload that results in movement in the counter direction.

Furthermore, when you apply force to a system that has recently been exposed to force, and is already out of balance, it's risky because that system is more vulnerable than it was before the first time it was hit. Such a system will react more profoundly to an action that in other situations would seem almost harmless.

Think about how you feel when someone comments on your work the first time and what you feel when they comment on an additional aspect right after that.

Do you remember the case study we analyzed under Simplicity? It was the case where the manager almost risked losing a few of his best professionals due to what we found to be direction and communication issues. Overdoing influence as a result of lacking the effect of time is just what happened there. The team was not functioning at a satisfactory level, so management implemented change; they inserted a new incentive plan. They waited, what they thought was a reasonable amount of time, and once they didn't see the change they expected, they applied another change to increase the chances of success....

I'm sure you can see how important it is to understand systems within the context of time. It's important whenever you look at any system, and it's vital when you look at any level of human systems.

Kind Excellence Tip #9
Time and Systemic Thinking

The plant in Jonathan's office was wilted, and he instantly recognized it needed some water. It's a nice break from his thoughts for a couple of minutes, so he goes on and waters it with a jug of water. By the end of the day it seems to Jonathan that the plant is still not picking up. "Hmm, that's strange," he thinks to himself. "I'll give it a bit more water, just in case."

When Jonathan comes back in the morning, there is still no improvement. In fact, a couple of days later the plant is starting to turn yellow on the edges of its beautiful green leaves.

What just happened here?

Jonathan noticed a problem and took action in order to correct it. So far so good. Then he waited what seemed to him like a reasonable amount of time and expected to see change. This is where we make the first mistake. We often anticipate a change to take place in far less time than the amount required for it. Then he watered it again, reinforcing the same action again to speed up results. The second and more fatal mistake: We see little improvement so we invest more energy—in the same direction—to speed up, but as we do we exaggerate the amount of energy needed, and we create the opposite negative response. Now the plant is over-watered and it's starting to rot. Furthermore, because the plant's starting point was under-balanced, it was too weak to recuperate from being over-watered and went straight to the other extreme without showing any signs of getting better anywhere in the process.

And since we're talking about human systems already, let's zoom in here for a moment a see where we started and where we want to go.

The goal of *Outswim the Sharks* isn't to just give you great skills. We started off by saying that we want you to maximize your human asset potential, and I claimed you can only achieve these superior results by practicing kindness alongside a superb bunch of core skills.

So far Systemic Thinking can be applied to any nonlinear, complex system to produce excellent results. There is nothing to identifying an activation codex, extracting meaning, using the subconscious and tension, or understanding the effects of time and space that requires kindness.

But from here on if you are not holding a kindness pass, the doors will not open. And the next segment is the hall of individual and team excellence, so you do not want to miss it.

Getting your team members to excel requires them to have the desire to excel. Without kindness there is no desire, you may get the skills in, but if there is no desire there is no change.

Read on.

Leading Human Systems to Excel

A ship is safe in harbor, but that's not what ships are for.
                                              —*John A. Shedd*

Let's see what we've got here.

By getting your team members to use Systemic Thinking you have most likely already increased their skill level significantly. They are now better at strategizing, prioritizing, making decisions, and innovating. But you are still miles away from maximizing their emotional and intellectual assets.

Why?

Because the human systems in your team, your employees, are complex non linear systems that are run by contradictions and repetitions, and some of their codex segments are dysfunctional.

That's right, you can and you should improve human systems if you want them to excel. And you're going to learn how to do it without getting a second degree in psychology. In fact you won't have to learn anything new here. We'll only use what we talked about so far.

Ready?

Let's go.

When it comes to human systems change confronts a unique challenge. Human systems are the only systems that need to change themselves. If you find a dysfunctional element in any other complex system you can most often replace it. Here it's out of your hands.

Leading people to excel is where you start shedding off things that do not work and duplicating the patterns that propel your team or individual team members to excel. It requires Receptiveness, seeing things as they truly are, Core Analysis, and Systemic Thinking skills. It requires all of the Kind Excellence skills and techniques because only when we combine all of them can we have a strong enough platform to sustain a willingness to change.

I'm a big believer in people, well most people anyway. I believe people can learn and change just like I think managers can and should practice consulting skills. I've seen it work over and over again. Provided that people are trained with Kind Excellence, they will almost always be willing to make the effort to put in more of themselves, expose their weaknesses and grow. This is where that desire flame we keep working hard to preserve is going to make a big difference.

This change process, the path of Kind Excellence, has its own structure. There is nothing new here; only things are organized to accommodate an excellence training program.

Using Systemic Thinking to Define What Needs to Change

Process, process, but not a vision in sight.
                                                    —*The Path of Least Resistance*

Once you start looking at systems small or large, and extract meaning, you are instantly going to draw conclusions. Finally, it's time to do something direct about improving results.

The most important question about judging human asset systems is finding what works and what is getting in the way. It's not about what you think is the right way, and it has nothing to do with how you would do things. You can now look at the system as a separate whole and evaluate what's working for it.

Going back to the new manager example from the previous chapter, it's not about how things worked in your last position, but about what works for the team you're leading now. Though you saw two different patterns of communication in both teams, you will still need to figure out whether having a team leader be less knowledgeable about the details of the project is effective or not. Perhaps it is beneficial or functional for the system to have this team leader know less for some reason. Defining a dysfunction is not done by considering what you think, it's about what works best for the system.

I believe team members and managers, who are presented with appropriate analytical skills and someone like you to openly talk to, are fully capable of knowing what works for them and what gets in their way. As you notice one of your employees isn't being as productive as you wish for them to be, I suggest you wait before jumping to any conclusions. The reasons you may be associating with the problem, what you interpret as the element that needs to change, could be only a part of the picture, or you could be way off.

Kind Excellence Tip #10
Looking for Inner Logic

Think of a detective trying to figure out the inner logic of a sophisticated thief. It's commonly a puzzle with many pieces that do not fit together to the observer, but the only way to unlock the crime is by revealing the inner logic behind the thefts.

Do note, the detective is not trying to figure out what the thief would do next, she is not trying to guess which house he'll choose next before figuring out the way his mind works. Neither does she think: "Oh well, if it was me I would choose that house instead."

You probably think I'm being silly. It's obvious isn't it?

Think again.

The first thing most of us do when we look at a system is judge it through our own lenses. We see a contradiction and immediately want to resolve it one way or another and establish the "truth," the "right thing." What do we think is wrong with this system? Why do we think it's not effective? What do we think needs to change?

That's nice, but it's not Systemic Thinking.

Human asset systems are hard to decipher, because they have inner conflicts, they are unpredictable, complex and dynamic. They are so hard to work with because people think, they have wants and subjective needs, oh, and they feel too. That's a real challenge, but it's also the biggest resource, the one benefit no other system can give you. Use it!

Why decide what is getting in a system's way if you can ask it?

I know, it's so damn easy,* you present the system (these are people we're talking about) with contradictions or repetitions

---

* In nonlinear complex systems that are not human systems you'll have to judge whether a pattern is dysfunctional by trying to link it to results over time. In a way you'll have to find the patterns this element has in respect to producing effective results.

and you ask them if it serves them or gets in their way. Now of course they won't always want to tell you right away, sometimes because they hate to admit it themselves and at times because they haven't figured it out, but we'll take care of that soon. If you're getting rejections that are based on other causes such as lack of trust or commitment, I suggest you go back to Simplicity and Real Knowledge, or consider that perhaps the individual you are working with does not belong in your team.

Good, now we know what needs to change, let's get our hands dirty.

Applying Change

You cannot go into the womb to form the child; it is there and makes itself and comes forth whole—and there it is and you have made it and have felt it, but it has come itself.
—*Gertrude Stein*

Changing human asset systems is a training plan. You work with an employee (or in other cases a team, a department or even an organization) to design a dynamic work program, tailor made, and adjustable to progress. Then you let them apply it, you adjust it, and facilitate change.

Kind Excellence Tip #11
Respecting the Place of Dysfunctions in Systems

Eastern philosophies view any system as a balance seeking whole. Any imbalance causes compensation in the rest of the system which is designed to balance the system to the best of its ability. So if you were to start leaning backward when you walk, your body would instantly regain its balance by moving your legs forward.

Now suppose you went to a guy that walked this way and forced him to reinstate his legs in their previous position without straightening his back. What do you think would happen?

In the same way, if your team, or one of your employees, exhibits a dysfunctional behavior, that behavior is linked to a bunch of other dysfunctional behaviors that have been created to help him live with himself. If, for instance, your employee is afraid of taking responsibility for his actions because he fears the consequences of such actions, he might use dysfunctional behaviors like lying or hiding failures.

And what do you think would happen if in your next review with this employee you would have confronted him with his hiding and maybe even lying behavior without removing his fear of bearing the consequences of his actions?

In both cases removing a secondary response to the cause will make them fall flat on their face.

*Incidentally, combining the understandings of time, space, and Systemic Thinking with this principle right here is the logic behind letting balance present itself gradually instead of forcing it on a situation. I am forever grateful to Amnon Katz, a one of a kind consultant, psychologist, and colleague who planted the seeds for these ideas in my mind.

It's that simple.

Let's take this step by step. Take a look at one of your employees for a moment.

This is an involved motivated team player that lets his actions do the talking. He is bright, innovative and is often the go-to person when it comes to professional questions. There is only one problem; he likes to go about doing things in a way that is often inefficient. You've noticed he hangs on to certain ways of doing things despite clear evidence to the fact that it slows his progress and the progress of his projects as a result.

Now, let's assume you have the complete trust of this wonderful employee. He is even willing to discuss things with you openly (which is a really why kindness works better than any other management style). Both of you discussed his system as you were building it from DNA segments, and you can now see very clearly that this behavior stems from investing energy to avoid others taking over. You use Core Analysis and you realize that the reason for this is that this wonderful creative employee doesn't feel he knows his own self worth.

Put your mind at ease. I'm not asking you to psychoanalyze this person. All you need to do is use Kind Excellence skills. There are no other skills required. Remember it's his conclusions to the contradictions and repetitions presented to him that lead him to these conclusions. The employee himself (or the team, or workgroups if you need to reflect the whole organization) is the one drawing reasons and causes. Your work just allows him to dig it out.

So far there's nothing new.

And guess what you should do now?

You do not do anything. This situation's tension should be treated by tension's rules.

Well… almost nothing anyway.

All you do is kindly, gently, and with the greatest amount of support and confidence in your employee's ability to change, highlight the results of this behavior whenever you notice them occur. An occasional: "Hey, look, you're doing it again!" is all it takes. No criticism please, just be the Jiminy Cricket in his pocket; that's all you are.

Your employees' desire to resolve tension, to improve in a safe and supportive environment will do the rest.

That's it, all of that work was to get here and do nothing?

Yes indeed, and for two very good reasons: placing responsibility where it needs to be and letting tension do its work itself.

Let's start from the latter. We've talked about tension and how its strongest desire is to resolve. When you present your employee, or other human asset systems such as teams or organizations, with a dissonance, a difference between two elements, the most natural reaction is a desire to eliminate that gap. You both need to agree that you want to resolve the dissonance, and you can only gain that through kindness. But then it is your job to keep tension alive to make change possible. Any other force thrown into the system, any pressure or wrong motivation is going to interfere with the natural forces of tension trying to resolve. Any deliberate attempt to give anything other than direction is going to create a counter reaction, resistance of some sort, and interfere with the work tension has to do.

We may want to resolve tension with everything we have, but if we do not understand tension, we're bound to reinforce the gap instead.

Think about it this way: You are fifteen, hungry but busy, and your mother is letting you know supper is ready. Now you are stalling a bit because you are in the middle of something and your mom is calling you again: "If you're not coming down in two minutes, I'm removing your plate from the table! I can't stand it that I work hard to cook your food and then you do not even show me the courtesy of showing up for dinner." Now a part of you feels you do not want to join her no matter how hungry you are.

What just happened?

Had your mom left the tension to resolve you would have come to the table soon enough, after all you are hungry and she cooks well. But applying additional force to resolve tension makes it more difficult and sometimes impossible for tension to resolve. There is something about tension, that if we try to push it to resolve it shuts things down.

In order to cash in on tension we need to work with tension according to tension's rules.

Do remind your human system that he should not try to change things forcefully, either. Your employee should not start by behaving differently. All he needs is to begin by making a conscious decision to change. As he tries to change, notice his regressions (going back to old patterns), wait and watch for resistance and keep investigating.

What you see before you here is that human systems are revealed in layers, and by building a system you are at times only exposed to some of the information. Like an archeological expedition, it's only once a certain layer has been discovered and clarified that we can even begin to see the deeper levels.

Remember that when we look at change it is vital to understand that things are a certain way for a reason. It might be the wrong reason, but there is a reason for things to be as they are. If you try to implement change without understanding the forces holding the situation as it is, you are probably not going to be successful. You have to assume that if you're keeping a mechanism it's because somewhere, in a very specific situation, on some level it makes sense to you. Without breaking the logic behind the need to practice something a certain way, you can't very well expect to see consistent change.

When it comes to helping others change, there is another good reason to do almost nothing: keeping responsibility where it belongs.

If you take it on to yourself to be responsible for change, your human system is going to relinquish some of the responsibility to you. A lesser sense of responsibility means lesser commitment, and you can start waving change and excellence goodbye.

I've seen this happen all the time. In my line of work I've seen so many managers fall in this trap. But even more, I've seen consultants fall in it. In fact, this very reason was one of my first motivations to create core skills in the first place. I wanted to give managers real skills because I think it's not only the right thing to do, but also the choice with the greater chance of success because the responsibility stays where it belongs. Do you see where I'm going here?

I'm almost ready to let you go on your merry way, but before you go, do not forget to get your practice.

Read on.

Chapter Eleven

Practice Systemic Thinking

I F YOU'RE STILL A little puzzled as to how to use Systemic Thinking, the case study before you should put things in place.

Systemic Thinking, as a thinking tool, is the same when applied at any level. I'm speeding you along to the level of mastery in this example so that your mind can start from the end and have a clear grasp on what needs to be achieved.

Systemic Thinking—Try It Out

Let's start looking at this challenge by getting our subconscious engaged here. Once we define the contradiction remember not to surrender tension to your conscious thoughts. The whole point is to get your mind to open up and wonder.

There's Nothing Like Experience
A Case Study

A large IT solutions company
Management team

In preparation for a corporate identity change, this company wisely decided to combine its marketing efforts with organizational change professional support.

> *The concept behind the marketing change was to overcome the conglomerate structure, and its perception in the eyes of the company's clients, creating an image of a system that could provide multiple solutions.*
>
> *In order to obtain information on how the company was perceived and how it should be perceived we held discussion groups of employees from different departments and other interest groups.*
>
> *The Facts:*
> * *Employees perceived the company as many sub companies. The images given to describe it were: octopus, a disassembled jigsaw puzzle, and a crossroad sign.*
> * *The reason for these problems according to surveys was a lack of formal and informal structures that connected the different departments.*
> * *When presented with ongoing updates the VP of marketing and the CEO focused on changing the perception of employees, throwing a big party, and distributing shirts, hats, and other gadgets, ignoring the messages staff brought them.*
> * *The staff came up with over 10 practical and inexpensive recommendations to improve this problem.*
> * *The CEO used none of the recommendations. He focused all of his change efforts on external marketing.*

Look at the following contradictions:

* A company that was built as a collection of different small independent companies is now trying to create a coherent whole. Mark the contradiction as past and future patterns.
* Making the change on the outside, but keeping everything the same on the inside.
* The CEO has dedicated money to research his employees' opinions, but made no use of those. Mark

the contradiction as producing something but not using it.

Now start looking for DNA segments in between and across these contradictions.

Is your brain scattered already? Feeling a little like reading the words over and over doesn't make them sink in?

Great, that's exactly where you need to be.

Here is what I see when I stare at these statements using my wandering state of mind.

I wonder why this CEO built the company that way to begin with. Why didn't he change it after the third sub company was created? I think this CEO is a builder and a doer. I think one of his DNA segments is that he doesn't plan things by looking at how things affect each other. In other words, I think this manager isn't using Systemic Thinking.

Looking at the second contradiction reinforces this understanding, and from repetition I can now see a pattern. Choosing to address marketing before managing change isn't just a matter of order here. It's fine to start with an image change and then plan to address inside issues. But it's a whole other thing to think that you can make people integrate a change by throwing a big party and handing off T-shirts and hats. That means that this CEO isn't using Simplicity skills either. He thinks he can facilitate change by investing time and money in symptoms. There is no core thinking here, and obviously no receptiveness. Here is another DNA segment.

Are you surprised that a big time CEO does not know how to use Systemic Thinking and Simplicity? Do not be. I wish this case was a fiction of my imagination. Unfortunately it's too common and very real. But wait, I'm digressing.

The final contradiction brings up yet another insight. This CEO is presenting one thing and doing another. While it would seem he is trying to get his team's input in order to make some use of it, in truth he has no intention of using it. Why is that I wonder?

Let's look at it some more. Now let's turn to look across contradictions. What does building the company into non-communicating sub-companies have in common with making the change appear only on the outside?

Can you feel the subconscious at work again? Let it go, it's doing what it's supposed to.

I could tell you what I think, but why don't you try it out. This is the pro's league, but you can do it.

This is a typical case in which all layers of the system are suffering from a core dysfunction. This CEO built an empire of services and capabilities in his organization, but without Systemic Thinking that's all he has—a dispatched group of units that hardly know of each other's existence not to mention function as a coherent system.

It's the same system DNA segment that manifests itself in each of the system's processes. You can look at any level of the system, any department, and you will find the same thing over and over again. While this CEO was aiming to change the organizational image to the company's customers, he could have benefited tremendously (as most of his staff easily recognized) from realizing that the same patterns existed within the organization.

The fact that different departments and teams knew very little about other departments and teams meant missing opportunities to offer clients a more comprehensive solution (reselling other solutions to satisfied customers can't be easier when you have so many options to choose from), offering valued employees more advancement options in place of those leaving as a result of having few promotion options in their own department. Furthermore, this resulted in an inadequate use of organizational resources in which departments are competing over resources instead of banking on synergy, a lack of alignment of goals, and much more.

Because the message of synergy feels hollow to employees, keeping it in their awareness is going to require investing continues energy. Teams that are not convinced the different parts of the system are connected, that are in fact confident the different parts are disconnected, are much less likely to sing the song of "use our organization's other services" to their clients.

And if they do this initiative, which is not backed up in reality, it is risky. Projecting to the world that an organization is made up of a well oiled machine in which different parts work smoothly together, while offering a machine in which each part works by itself is bound to backfire. Expectations that are not met lead to disappointment which leads to frustration and results in losing customers.

What you can see if you look closely across the different contradictions is that this very successful manager is a typical shark. He wants things done his way, and he'll try to force reality to obey his vision. It's obviously worked for him in the past, and it will probably continue to work for him in the future as long as he keeps making the company grow. But it is short sighted because of two reasons. Firstly he could gain even more without losing any of it by practicing Kind Excellence skills, that's obvious. But even more importantly in this case, once this company reaches a plateau, (which it did; that's the reason the CEO is turning to improving what he already has), it won't be able to get to the next level. Without using Systemic Thinking and Simplicity, which requires the use of Real Knowledge, and without practicing kindness this director can not improve.

A real revolution begins when you understand that true long term excellence can't exist without kindness.

Systemic Thinking—Maximizing Human Assets

As a manager, Systemic Thinking is crucial. Simply put, there is no management without integration, and there is no integration without Systemic Thinking.

So when it comes to management development, Systemic Thinking is the ultimate skill. It starts when you work on developing management potential at the employee level, it goes on to boost the performances of beginners and finally fine tune the skills of executives.

It is an incredibly vital skill for management development because it embodies additional skills. Systemic Thinking is the only skill that can train managers in strategizing (decision making, evaluating different alternatives, and choosing the most effective course of action), managing priorities, identify threats and opportunities, problem solving and innovation. All of these depend on the ability to integrate, and once the ability to find a connection that wasn't there before increases, these skills get an instant boost.

Note that Kind Excellence training is not training in prioritizing, strategizing, and innovation. But by giving you the core skill that is at the heart of all these, these quickly become a by product.

Systemic Thinking and Building Up a Desire to Excel

The goal of Systemic Thinking is creating well balanced, functional systems. When it comes to human asset systems, balanced individuals and balanced teams are happy individuals and teams.

Practicing Systemic Thinking means removing many of the inner contradictions and dysfunctional patterns a system is suffering from which directly leads to a more harmonious flow of things. Employees come to work and feel better about themselves because they experience their inner contradictions as a source of growth rather than a source of frustration.

Once upon a time when I had to give feedback it was an unpleasant experience. Now feedback, even on the most difficult of topics, is often funny. Who would have believed that feedback and highlighting dysfunctional elements could be a factor that increases the desire to excel?

Working with your team on their dysfunctional elements through Systemic Thinking techniques is a training plan. When people know exactly what they need to improve on an individual, team, and organizational level, and how to go about it, improvement is the natural next step. Procrastination, a lack of follow up, an inability to evaluate your load taking on too many tasks without integrating slack time, and not thinking a project trough to its completion are but a few good examples of dysfunctional behaviors that Systemic Thinking can help your staff get rid of.

And getting rid of contradicting values and dysfunctions is as uplifting for a team.

A team that experiences the contradictions between its members as a positive potential will have less conflicts, and will function with more synergy. Like playing harmoniously in an orchestra, it's a great feeling to be part of. Engaging in this ongoing dialogue through differences means people constantly negotiate questions such as: Why are we doing this? This and other such questions are shared vision builders. A shared vision and a mutual sense of direction provide people with purpose and purpose increases the desire to excel.

Furthermore, Systemic Thinking is the basic ingredient for creative thinking.* People who practice Systemic Thinking on a regular basis enjoy resolving challenges, but they also enjoy the company of their creative self waking up to life. Just look at the literature—creative expression is by far the strongest intrinsic motivator you can offer your team.

People who think creatively maximize their ability to think. It exercises their mind and makes it possible to use a larger capacity of it. Using Systemic Thinking means that people have an opportunity to grow professionally and personally. This ability to show one's skills, to do better, is the base for satisfaction. It's not the work, the interest and personal gain (in terms of knowing and learning more) that makes people more committed to the organization, but rather the fact that they feel they fulfill themselves. People, who experience themselves as more capable, feel more confident in their ability to maximize their potential. When consultants and managers talk about empowerment, it is really that experience of being more capable they are trying to achieve.

Systemic Thinking and the Skills to Excel

In the marketing department a team leader is trying to motivate her team. One of your employees, one of the experts in your development team, is trying to design a chip that will be superior to other competing products. In a different department three

---

* That's because creative thinking is brought about by making new connections between existing ideas, and Systemic Thinking is the super power tool for helping make those connections.

staff members realize that the latest market changes are going to require a speedy response in order to seize a unique opportunity. Each one of these has to incorporate an ocean of information, often in a dynamic environment with many unknown factors. Clearly these employees are experts in their field, you know that. What you were less aware of until today is the fact that each one of them is also skilled in using Systemic Thinking.

Systemic Thinking skills apply to almost any nonlinear, complex system. It is imperative for any type of thinking process that requires integration so that includes prioritizing, strategizing, decision making, innovation, project management, and team aspects. And finally, it is at the heart of self improvement. It provides the skills required in order to remove dysfunctional mechanisms and lead a system to balance.

Systemic Thinking is great for any kind of nonlinear, complex systems—Systemic Thinking is not limited to human systems. Once you master the techniques they will be as effective for balancing and finding DNA segments of any nonlinear complex system (with the exception of chaotic systems). You can use Systemic Thinking to balance and find the DNA segments of a project, integrate market fluctuations to choose an investment option, invent a new product, look at the organizational structure, and much more. And the beauty of it is that once you master the technique, you'll start integrating this new way of thinking into everything you do spontaneously.

Think about it this way: by learning how to think differently you'll change your own system's DNA, and like any good DNA segment, it will manifest itself in anything you do.

Improving decision making, strategizing, and prioritizing—
When you try to make a decision, choose a strategy, or
prioritize, you need to gather all the information you can about
the challenge you're facing, extract meaning, set up different
solution alternatives, and finally choose the optimal solution.

That's just a standard decision making process.

But that's just the structure, the skeleton of the process. The
thinking process that supports all of these skills is Systemic
Thinking. Without it there is no integration, and without
integration none of these will lead to effective results.

Furthermore, in order to make sound decisions, prioritize, and
strategize, you need to consider how a change in one place of
a system is going to affect the rest of the system. Without that
you'll keep trying to improve things, to find that you have caused
damage in other places of the system.

Being able to predict or stay alert to the possible implications
of a decision increases the chances that decision leads to success.
If you are capable of predicting your competition's responses to
your marketing strategy, you will be a better marketer. When
you are developing a new product, knowing that a change in the
old design is going to require additional changes, and predicting
what those changes are going to be, will help you work faster
through the project. A lack of Systemic Thinking can prove to
be very expensive. Not taking into account the implications of
encouraging your staff to work long hours without break, or have
long days, may result in poor performances or increased turnover.
If you hire two new employees just when your department is
approaching a deadline, without taking into account that new
team members require training time, then you are going to reduce
your productivity at the time you need it at its peak. And these
are but small examples.

Systemic Thinking is required for building a mission and an organizational vision, choosing which vendor you will hire, and even choosing an approach for a feedback session. All of these require an ability to make decisions, integrate and choose which are at the heart of Systemic Thinking.

You can either let your staff learn how to control decision making, and other strategic skills as a deliberate process, or just let chance do what it does best.

Sharpening innovation skills— In its essence innovation is the ability to integrate old things into something new. Sounds familiar? When creativity experts talk about innovation and creativity skills they throw out terms like: suspended judgment, stop and go, puzzles, paradox, and alternatives.

It is not accidental that all of these have been mentioned in part four. Among creativity techniques you'll find variations of the bouncing techniques we discussed earlier, different versions of puzzles and paradoxes that are meant to exercise the creative parts of your brain.

But now you know much more than techniques, you know why these techniques work. Like Systemic Thinking creativity is a skill that can only be awaken through subconscious thinking. You now know how to work with tension, and why being stuck is just another aspect of creative thinking. With this arsenal of core skills, your creative thinking is not limited to practicing puzzles. You can now apply this wonderful way of thinking to anything, increase your skills fast and develop independence in using it in no time at all.

Improving the players themselves— *Outswim the Sharks* is about the skills required to maximize your team's intellectual and emotional assets through kindness. Getting people to excel has to include improving the performances and harnessing more of what people can offer to get the job done.

With that goal in mind we can't ignore the lead players themselves. And the players, well, they're almost never perfect. Nearly any human system has some dysfunctions. But if you help the system get rid of its dysfunctions, the system becomes more effective and more efficient, and in the case of human systems, more content. If you do not, the system will spend much of its energy bouncing back and forth trying unsuccessfully to resolve an impossible combination.

It's a simple idea.

It is hence vital to see things in context and so Systemic Thinking becomes imperative when it comes to maximizing human assets. Without understanding how their own human system functions, employees won't be able to improve as individuals or as a team.

And just like systemic thinking works to improve individuals, it is essential for developing skills to improve team work and projects.

Systemic Thinking: Test Yourself

- *When I try to understand a system, I let my subconscious funnel through all of the information to identify the most significant factors.*

- *When in disagreement, I look for the reason that connects both ends instead of choosing one end over the other.*

- *I treat my subconscious thinking as a legitimate type of thinking and use it to my benefit.*

- *Whenever I have an opportunity to look for commonalities in contradictions or repetitions and create systems, I do so.*

- *I am familiar with each team member's strengths and personal challenges, and I use both to enhance the potential of my team.*

- *When I am faced with tension, I use it as an opportunity to increase growth.*

- *Once I identify how a system needs to change I present the dissonance and step aside supportively.*

- *I let change take its time.*

- *When I need to change something, I try to research how it will affect others.*

- *I don't try to remove dysfunctions. I know they are there for a reason so I try to remove their cause instead.*

- *Systemic Thinking is best practiced constantly. I take any opportunity I get.*

That's it, my friend. It's a wrap. I've given you everything I could so that you can quickly develop the basic level of Kind Excellence skills independently of my support. If you do the same for your staff, I sincerely believe we'll all live in a much better world. Teach yourself. Then mentor them. They'll make you look good. I promise you!

Part V

- Straight to the Point
- The First Skill of Kind Excellence—Real Knowledge
- The Second Skill of Kind Excellence—Simplicity
- The Third Skill of Kind Excellence—Systemic Thinking
- **CONCLUSION**

Conclusion

Healing the universe is an inside job.

—Fred Kofman

NOW IT'S JUST YOU and me. There are no more techniques, models, theories, and skills. Just two people talking.

Tell me, what makes you happy?

I'll take any answer and if your happiness doesn't include hurting others or yourself I won't be judgmental.

I ask myself this question everyday. I think of myself as if I was at my death's bed wondering how I lived my life in retrospect.

It's funny, you know. I've been practicing kindness all this time, struggling to stay authentic in the harshest segment of this world. I've been going back to the sharks with the message of kindness. Was it a waste of my time? Is there any point to it?

What's the alternative though? Preaching to the choir isn't really helping here. It only reinforces the two extremes. I keep going back in the dangerous waters because I do not see kindness as a touchy feely, all about giving to others approach. I see kindness, as long as it's genuine and accompanied by the right skills, as the best money making solution.

It's hard to tell why that is really.

I managed to go through a whole book that has kindness in its subtitle without defining kindness. I have no intention of changing that now. I know that kindness isn't this weak attribute (that's why you can find all these books about the power of nice and the power of kindness, which include wonderful definitions of kindness in case you're interested). Kindness is a practical approach to life. Anyone who knows me or has used Kind Excellence techniques will tell you that.

It's Story Time
The Puzzle of Life (source unknown)

A scientist was trying to get some work done, when suddenly his five-year-old son approached him. The young boy was determined to help his father with his work. When the scientist saw he could not persuade the child to leave the room, he decided to find something to keep his son busy. Looking around, the scientist saw a magazine, one of the many that was scattered on his desk, and started flipping through it to find a picture of the globe. He tore it out, cut it to small pieces, and handed it to the boy with some tape.

"You like puzzles, right? Take these pieces of the world, and let's see if you can put them together all by yourself."

The scientist thought it would take his son a good while to play with the pieces when only moments later the boy returned with a reconstructed picture of the globe clutched in his small hand.

"I can't believe it!" the scientist exclaimed. "This must be the first time you've seen a picture of the globe. How did you do it?"

"Daddy," the child replied, "I didn't know what the world looks like, but when you tore the page out of the magazine I saw that on the other side of the page there was a picture of a man. At first, I tried to fix the picture of the world like you asked. But then I thought it would be better to turn the page over and put the pieces of the man together instead. When I turned the paper over, I saw that by fixing the man, I managed to fix the world."

Personally I believe all the spiritual pursuit of kindness is doing all of us a disservice. People associate kindness with giving endlessly, with presenting the other cheek. To me there is nothing further from the truth.

I'm not going to stand here telling you it's easy, I should know better. But I will tell you that from my experience the only thing that is standing in your way isn't what you might think it is. It's not the other people who choose anything but kindness, it's not the world of business that dictates shark mentality, if anything is standing in your way it's you.

Start with you.

But do it right. Do it so that you can become another living example that kindness isn't weak. Show everyone around you that if you practice kindness with the right set of skills, it reaches superior results.

Whatever your reasons for doing it, I salute you.

Here is to your success.

Acknowledgments

If I've ever been able to give it's only because I've been able to receive.
—*Reut Schwartz-Hebron*

A BOOK IS LIKE AN ocean filled by the waters of rivers, streams, and creeks. It's very hard to tell where it begins. I am grateful to all of my friends and foes for enlightening me.

I am very appreciative of the trust and passion for cooperation that have been bestowed on me by clients. I truly appreciate how quickly you have allowed me and my techniques into your professional and personal lives.

A special thanks to Dalia Katz-Ganin and Dafna Liber. Both believed in me more than I believed in myself when I just started this journey. One can't ask for better friends.

I would also like to thank Lisa Rojany Buccieri for her wonderful editing and Tamar Nahir Yanai for the cover design and for being a source of endless support. To my dear friend Hanina Stettin, who is 75 in years of wisdom with the enthusiasm saved for the young, my respect and gratitude.

I thank my parents for choosing to invest their money in taking my brother and I all over the world as children, exposing me to values, and letting me choose my own.

Most of all, I humbly thank my husband for being the best friend anyone can ask for and for choosing to adjust with me through the tides of change.